, Mary McMahon, Mary McMaho

Don Bosco: a Sketch of his Life and Miracles

, Mary McMahon, Mary McMaho

Don Bosco: a Sketch of his Life and Miracles

ISBN/EAN: 9783743343597

Manufactured in Europe, USA, Canada, Australia, Japa

Cover: Foto ©ninafisch / pixelio.de

Manufactured and distributed by brebook publishing software (www.brebook.com)

, Mary McMahon, Mary McMaho

Don Bosco: a Sketch of his Life and Miracles

Maria auxilium christianorum
ora pro nobis

abbé Jean Bosco

Don Bosco:

A Sketch of

His Life and Miracles.

BY

Dr. Charles D'Espiney.

TRANSLATED FROM THE FRENCH BY

MISS MARY McMAHON.

"*Praise be to Our Lady Help of Christians.*"

SECOND EDITION.

NEW YORK, CINCINNATI, AND ST. LOUIS:
BENZIGER BROTHERS,
Printers to the Holy Apostolic See.
1885.

The Author's Protest.

In attempting to relate some of the graces and favors obtained through the intercession of Our Lady Help of Christians, the author wishes to conform always and in all things to the decisions of Our Holy Mother the Church, and particularly to the decrees of His Holiness Pope Urban VIII.

Copyright, 1883, by Benziger Brothers.

CONTENTS.

	PAGE
Don Bosco	9
The Coöperators of St. Francis de Sales	82
The Devotion to Our Lady Help of Christians	89
A Cure	99
A Medal of Our Lady Help of Christians	100
The Incredulous Physician	104
The Gold Bracelet	106
Miraculous Cure of a Sick Man	108
Cure of a General	113
A Cripple	117
Cure of a Sick Woman, and the Conversion of a City	121
A Vocation and Cure	125
How Count C. entered Holy Orders at the Age of Sixty-three	127
Providence is a Good Banker	131
An Opportune Clap of Thunder	138

CONTENTS.

	PAGE
A Charitable Spirit	139
A Bargain	140
How Our Lord punished the Ingratitude shown to Don Bosco, and those who tried to thwart him	141
What came of an Attempt to put Don Bosco in an Insane Asylum	145
The Colonel	149
How Don Bosco managed to take the Young Culprits in the Prison of Turin out for a Holiday	151
The Seminarian Francis	154
A Sick Friend	155
A Confession	157
A Dream	158
Piety of Don Bosco's Children	161
The Attempts to Kill Don Bosco	164
Don Bosco's Dog	170
The Confession of a Thief	178
Don Bosco, *a Poem*	180

DON BOSCO.

"TENDER love for his neighbor is one of the greatest and most excellent gifts that Divine Providence can bestow upon man."

The spirit of these charming words of St. Francis de Sales, inscribed at the head of the Salésian Bulletin, is truly characteristic of this work and the man of this work.

No one can see Don Bosco without feeling attracted to him, or without loving him at once, for his heart is all love, and the divine light of a tender love beams in his countenance.

Like St. John, the beloved disciple, leaning on the heart of the Master, inebriated with ineffable delight and exclaiming: "Lord, I love Thee," so Don Bosco, taking to his heart this multitude of children to whom he became a father, sends forth a sigh of love which assuredly ascends to the feet of Him who said, "This is My commandment, that you love one another as I have loved you."

The Abbé Don Bosco founded the Society of St. Francis de Sales, the object of which is to devote itself to the different works of piety and charity, and in particular to *the special care of poor abandoned children* upon whom depends the future happiness or misery of society.

Poor abandoned children! Could there be a more admirable work than that of *taking special care* of children whom neglect, ignorance, and contact with depraved, perverted natures defencelessly expose to the snares of evil?

Don Bosco gathers them together, gives them an asylum, teaches them an honorable trade, makes them useful citizens; but above all, he ennobles them, as it were, by initiating them in the splendors of revealed truth. He teaches them how to appreciate the immortal beauty of that soul made in the image of God, which they outrage through ignorance. Many of these children of the people have been raised to the highest dignity with which man can be invested: they have become priests!

We shall see how Don Bosco received the first inspiration of the mission which Divine Providence was to confide to him.

Elevated to the priesthood in 1841 at the age of twenty-six, instead of accepting the places offered to him he resolved to remain for a time at Turin under the immediate guidance of his compatriot and spiritual director, the Abbé Cafasso, then President of the Conference of Morals and Director of the Ecclesiastical Institute of St. Francis of Assisi.

Don Bosco had unbounded confidence and veneration for this worthy priest. He submitted to him all his actions and deliberations, and entered this Institute, the object of which was to perfect young priests in the knowledge of practical morals, and in the exercise of preaching.

The influence of this house was most favorable to the expansion of the soul; the inmates studied, but above all they prayed: yet this did not exclude an active participation in exterior works of charity, such as visiting the poor, the sick, the hospitals and prisons.

Don Bosco was introduced by his master into the prisons of Turin. The young priest was deeply moved at finding in the prisons great numbers of young boys, and even children.

He was filled with horror and pity at their precocious depravity, the cause of which was too evident, as from their birth these poor children were completely abandoned, and had always before their eyes a deplorable example of vice. They broke the law, and society, considering them injurious to the community, must needs imprison them. But far from bettering their condition, their sojourn in prison only rendered them still more corrupt.

From that time he labored unceasingly, impelled by an invisible impulse to devote himself to the poor abandoned children who crowded the streets of Turin. He resolved to snatch them from the evil influences to which they were a prey, and to teach them to know, love, and serve the God who died for them and of whom they had never heard. While contemplating this great object which he had so much at heart, an unforeseen circumstance, or rather the hand of God Himself, brought him his first neophyte, Barthelemy Garelli d'Asti, an orphan sixteen years old, who, like so many others, lived abandoned in the streets of Turin.

He entered by chance the sacristy of the church where Don Bosco was vesting for Mass, and the sacristan, who was at that moment looking for some one to serve the Mass, readily seized the boy.

Garelli was at a loss how to render such a service, and as he refused to comply with the somewhat blunt request, the sacristan gave him a sound box on the ear, which made him cry out.

Don Bosco was attracted by the noise and disturbance, and when informed of the cause he comforted and petted the boy and coaxed him to remain and hear Mass, after which he talked with him, asking him many questions.

He was horrified at the boy's perfect ignorance of the first rudiments of religion, and that same evening began his religious education by teaching him the sign of the Cross.

Thus was the *Œuvre Salésienne* begun on the beautiful feast of the Immaculate Conception of the Blessed Virgin, the 8th of December, 1841.

O Queen of Heaven! what graces have you not obtained since then for Don Bosco and his children!

Having noticed the effect of harsh treatment on the first child sent him by Providence, Don Bosco was from that moment fully convinced that children should always be treated with extreme gentleness. This exquisite gentleness, amounting even to tenderness, has become the motto and spirit of the Salésian Society.

The instruction in catechism given to Garelli soon attracted several of his comrades, and though mostly masons' apprentices, bound when very young to masters who took no care of them, it is worthy of notice that from this time none of the children fell victims to those accidents so frequent in their rude and perilous trade. At the beginning of the year 1842 Don Bosco found himself in charge of a hundred children and youths, to whom he taught the principles of religion. He collected them together as often as possible, and took them to Mass and Vespers. He even succeeded, but with some difficulty, in forming a small choir, whose singing added much to the attraction of the reunions. When he could, he never failed to procure for them some material gratification. He also visited them in their workshops, and when he found any of them out of employment he scoured the country till he found them good masters.

The Institute of St. Francis of Assisi, with its modest chapel and adjoining sacristy, was the first asylum offered to these children. From the beginning Don Bosco gave to the reunions the name of the *Oratory*, thus markedly showing that prayer was the sole power upon which he relied; he also from the commencement placed himself and all his children under the immediate protection of the Blessed Virgin.

In 1844, when Don Bosco, having finished his studies at the Institute of St. Francis of Assisi, was now about to assume the more decided duties of the priesthood, several positions were offered to him, but as usual, wishing to give up his own will, he confided this important decision to his director, the

Abbé Cafasso, whom he considered as the interpreter of the Divine Will in his regard.

His inclinations led him to devote himself more and more to the children whom he loved with a *tender love*, but, with a detachment worthy of admiration, he was willing to go wherever Almighty God sent him. After much prayer and reflection, the Abbé Cafasso appointed him director of the little hospital of St. Philomena. He assisted also in the direction of a Refuge for young girls, established in the neighborhood by the Marquise Barolo.

This new position seemed at first entirely incompatible with the development of the little Oratory, but it was really most favorable to it.

In the Abbé Borel, a priest of French origin, then director of the Refuge, Don Bosco found a friend such as Almighty God gives only to His elect, and one who proved an incomparable aid in the work for the children. As soon as these two priests met, it seemed as if they had always known each other; their love was mutual, and they went resolutely to work like old friends.

The little room allotted to Don Bosco at

the Refuge was the meeting-place for the children, who soon numbered more than two hundred. As the place was absolutely incapable of accommodating all, they filled the stairs and halls, and the state to which Don Bosco's poor little cell was reduced may be imagined. But a more serious grievance was that, even with the assistance of the Abbé Borel, he could not manage to hear all their confessions on the eve of certain feasts.

In this dilemma he applied to the Archbishop Franzoni, who approved and blessed the work. At this high recommendation the Marquise Barolo hastened to place at their disposition two rooms in the hospital, which they converted as best they could into a chapel. Here, on the 8th of December, 1844, the feast of the Immaculate Conception, Don Bosco said Mass for the first time, surrounded by his children. The work advanced under the manifest action of Divine Providence. At this time Don Bosco gave his Oratory the title of St. Francis de Sales.

He was guided in this choice by several circumstances. The material one was that the Marquise Barolo, having intended to found a congregation of priests under this title, had destined the very rooms which she gave to the Oratory for this purpose, and with this idea she had a picture of St. Francis de Sales painted at the entrance. In the second place, Don Bosco had long since recognized the unalterable sweetness and exquisite gentleness of St. Francis de Sales as the surest means of reaching the hearts of children. Moreover, several heresies had noiselessly glided into the city of Turin and threatened to disturb the faith of the people.

The work then became *The Oratory of St. Francis de Sales*, and this is why the family of Don Bosco bears the name *Salésian*.

But in order to rest on solid basis, all foundations must pass through trials and even persecution; for the road of the Cross is the only one that leads to life and truth.

These trials and persecutions were all the more sad and painful that they were sometimes instigated by wealthy people, and even by good Christians. Alas! the surest friendships are not always to be trusted: it is the old story, constantly repeated, of St. Peter denying his Master. We will show how this opposition manifested itself, and how Don Bosco bore himself through these difficulties.

The Oratory of St. Francis de Sales began to be definitely established. Catechism, singing of the canticles, instructions, interspersed with striking examples, interesting stories, and various games, filled the time of the reunions. Besides this, Don Bosco established night schools, which were soon attended by numerous adults, who after their day's work received elementary instruction very valuable to them.

But just at this time the Marquise Barolo reclaimed the place she had lent them, which she wished to use for another object. Don Bosco, through the Archbishop, obtained from the municipality the use of the Church of St. Martin.

This place was not very suitable for their purpose. Mass could not be celebrated in the church, which had long been abandoned, and there was no place for recreation except a small park in front of the church. Nevertheless the Oratory was transferred to the place assigned it, and we give here the memorable words of the Rev. Abbé Berol on this occasion: "My children, cabbages will not grow into fine large heads unless they are transplanted; it is then for our good that we are transplanted here." This good was not very apparent, but the ill-fortune was cheerfully accepted.

Three hundred children at play are noisy: it could hardly be otherwise. The people who lived in the houses facing the park which had become the playground, were soon annoyed by this unusual racket, they entered a complaint, and the municipal authorities notified Don Bosco that he would have to go elsewhere.

The municipality, however, far from being hostile to this work, even showed interest in the establishing of the night classes, and readily accorded Don Bosco the use of the church of *St. Pierre-ès-Liens*. Adjoining this church, so appropriate to the religious ceremonies, was a vast court just suitable as playground for the children, and a large vestibule served as a study-room, so that this change seemed for the best.

Alas! the next morning the rector who occupied the parsonage, annoyed by the noise of the children, and fearing the quiet he enjoyed in this retreat might be disturbed, made such a bitter complaint that the permission granted was immediately withdrawn.

Meeting in Don Bosco's cell was utterly impossible, and for two months the Oratory had to hold all its exercises in the open air.

On Sundays and feast days from early morning the children in great numbers gathered around Don Bosco, the new Moses, who conducted his little people to some church in the outskirts of the town, where he said Mass for them. Each one brought some provisions—not a repast of three courses, it is true, nor did they have three meals a day, but their appetites were incomparable. After a summary breakfast they had Catechism in the open air, and then instruction. They finished the day by a promenade, and returned in the evening to the city singing canticles, awaiting the promised land under the form of some sort of shelter.

This existence, full of sentiment from a

certain point of view, became impossible as the cold season approached. At the beginning of winter Don Bosco had to rent three rooms in the Moretta House, situated almost in front of the place where now stands the sanctuary of Our Lady Help of Christians.

But the time of rest had not yet come, and impediments to the work constantly occurred one after another.

First, the Marquis de Cavour, then chief of the municipal police of Turin, pretended to see in these inoffensive reunions a political object, dangerous to the state. He wished to have them suppressed, and all the energy of Don Bosco was needed to escape this serious difficulty.

Even the clergy of Turin joined Cavour's party. Some of them saw with jealousy a work established in which they had no share, and the curés claimed that their churches would be deserted.

The reply to this was very simple: since nearly all these children were strangers in the city, the greater part of them having neither hearth nor home, they consequently belonged to none of the parishes. Was it then a crime to withdraw them from the dangers of the street, and thus make valuable recruits for the Church?

This misunderstanding was no sooner settled than the lodgers in the Moretta House, where they held their meetings, complained so much of the noise made by the children, and of the inconvenience they caused, that the landlord rudely dismissed them, and they were once more in the street. This was in the spring of 1846, and the weather was beautiful. "Almighty God," thought Don Bosco, "treats my poor little children as well as He does the little birds." Not being able to find a house, he rented a meadow.

The Installation was so primitive at this time, that it forcibly recalled Our Lord wandering through the small towns of Judea, followed by His disciples, and with only the starry vault of heaven for shelter.

On Sunday the children came early, and began the day by going to confession to *their Father;* and certainly the mode of confession used in the Salésian family reminded one by its touching simplicity of the relation between father and son.

The priest's seat was a grassy mound; beside him knelt the little penitent, the arm of the priest lovingly encircling the child, while its head rested upon his heart. How sweet and easy the avowal of faults thus became!

Having no bell, the young battalion was assembled by a drum and trumpet found nobody knew where, and which would have delighted a lover of antiques. All the rest of the installation was to come. But what good he accomplished in this humble asylum! what charming, touching instructions penetrated the hearts of the children! What earnest and fervent prayers ascended to heaven!

The children were first taken to a neighboring church to hear Mass; then they breakfasted as best they could, and returned and spent the day in this pleasant meadow of Valdoco, where lively games judiciously alternated with instructions and spiritual exercises.

Alas! Don Bosco was soon unfortunately deprived of this meadow. The owner claimed that the tramping of the children destroyed the roots of the grass, and he notified them that they must leave.

The better to prove the instability of all human support, Don Bosco just at this time lost his position of Director to the Institute of the Marquise Barolo, and the emoluments thereof which were almost his only resource.

When this occurred, his friends and even Rev. Abbé Borel urged him to give up his care of the children. "Keep only twenty of the smaller ones and send the others away: you cannot accomplish impossibilities," they said; "and Divine Providence Himself seems clearly to indicate to you that the work is no longer to continue." "Divine Providence!" replied Don Bosco, raising his hands to heaven, while his eyes shone with surprising brilliancy, "sent me these children, and believe me, I will never send one away. I am firmly convinced that He will provide all that is necessary to them, and since I cannot rent a home, I will build one with the aid of Our Lady Help of Christians. We will have large buildings, capable of receiving as many children as will come; we will have all kinds of workshops, that they may learn whatever trade they wish; large courts and gardens for them to play in; finally, we will have a chapel and numerous priests to instruct the children, and to take special care of those among them who show signs of a religious vocation."

At this time it was supposed that Don Bosco had partially lost his reason; he was looked upon and pitied as one demented. This idea was confirmed by the minute description which he gave of his future Oratory, the plan of which evidently existed in his mind. He gave the description and dimensions of the chapel, the workshops, the dormitories, the class-rooms, the courts and gardens; and all conceived in proportions so vast and so little in keeping with his resources, that his mental derangement seemed no longer doubtful.

His friends gradually fell off; even those who seemed the most devotedly attached to him left him.

This belief in his mental aberration became so confirmed that they wished to confine him in an insane asylum.

We shall see later how the effort to carry out this idea resulted in the confusion of those who attempted it.

The day arrived when the children were to assemble for the last time in the meadow. The next morning it was to be given up to the owner, and Don Bosco knew not where he could assemble his dear little ones on the following Sunday.

It was like the Station at the Garden of Olives. Their countenances expressed deep dejection, and their cheeks bore traces of bitter tears.

The children saw him prostrate on the earth, and heard him cry out, "My God, may Thy holy will be done! Wilt Thou abandon these orphans? Inspire me how to find an asylum for them!"

Scarcely had he finished this prayer when a man named Pancrazio Soave approached him and asked, "Monsieur l'Abbé, are you looking for a laboratory?"

"Not a laboratory, but an oratory."

"No matter; I have what you want. My godfather, Pinardi, who is a very honest fellow, has a splendid shed to rent, exactly what you want."

What a providential opening! Don Bosco hastened with Pancrazio to the place indicated.

The shed was a structure of rare simplicity; no missionary among the savages could possibly have a ruder or more comfortless abode. The roof was so low that in certain parts one could not stand up without stooping, and the adjoining buildings were scarcely any better.

"It is certainly very low," said Don Bosco. "My children are not very tall, but they would find it difficult to lodge here."

"Is that all?" replied Pinardi. "I can have the soil dug down as deep as you wish; I will make a board floor, and you will have a little palace. Know, too, that I am a singer, and I will assist you by chanting at the services. I also have a beautiful lamp which I will lend you for your chapel."

Touched by such good-will, Don Bosco asked, "Could you lower the floor a foot and a half?"

"I will see that it is done."

"By next Sunday?"

"By next Sunday."

"You will allow me the use of the surrounding grounds?"

"You can have the use of them."

"How much?"

"Three hundred francs a year."

"I will give you three hundred and twenty francs, but I must have a lease."

"I will give you a lease."

"Then I will take it."

The affair concluded, Don Bosco returned to his meadow, and the setting sun lit up a very touching scene.

The poor children learned with great delight that Divine Providence had provided for them an asylum, and heartily cheered this shed of Valdoco which they were never to leave; for on this very spot was afterward built the Oratory of St. Francis de Sales as it now stands. They immediately repeated the Rosary in thanksgiving, and there could be no doubt of the fervor with which it was said.

Pinardi, assisted by Pancrazio and several workmen, accomplished wonders. In a week, as he had promised, the shed was made much more presentable, and on the following Sunday, the 12th of April, 1846 (it was Easter Sunday), they not only took possession of their new place, but were able to celebrate Mass and Vespers there. The shed, the floor of which had been lowered and covered with boards, made, with the addition of a coach-house, quite a good chapel, and all the adjoining ground served as playground for the children. The Bishop at once gave permission to say Mass and have all the religious exercises, Benediction, sermons, and novenas in the chapel. Soon there were seven hundred children in the Oratory of St. Francis de Sales du Valdoco, and the work took a decidedly encouraging start.

This success brought back to Don Bosco several friends who had recently deserted him, and attracted to him new assistants and valuable adherents.

The days were well filled at the Oratory. On Sundays and feast-days the chapel was open not only to the children, but to all in the neighborhood, who eagerly flocked to the modest chapel, which proved a blessing to this locality, inhabited by a very depraved class. An unhoped-for transformation may be said to have dated from this time.

Confessions were heard till eight or nine

o'clock in the morning; then Mass was said, Don Bosco always preaching a very interesting sermon on the Gospel of the day, adding examples taken from Sacred Scripture.

Then came recreation, followed by a class till noon. At two o'clock, Catechism, the Rosary, Vespers of the Blessed Virgin, another instruction, and singing of the Canticles.

All this was made so attractive, that when evening came the children were very loath to go away, and it was necessary to turn them out. They went off, calling "Good-by, Father; good-by till Sunday."

The good Don Bosco was generally so exhausted by his labors that he could scarcely drag himself home: but his strength seemed to be renewed by labor; so he hastened to definitely establish the night-school, which he kept open every night in the week.

The young men attended in large numbers; the great difficulty was to find teachers to help him with the classes.

This great need inspired Don Bosco with the ingenious idea of creating *scholarships*.

He selected the most talented young men, and offered to give them a complete course of instruction on condition that they would in their turn teach others.

Teaching is one of the best means of learning, and this institution of scholarships succeeded beyond all expectation.

He not only thus secured excellent and zealous teachers for his classes, but they became themselves a nursery of young priests, vocations developing among them at the same time with their instruction.

Don Bosco deserves much praise for the establishment of these night-schools; Turin and several other cities recognizing their excellence, hastened to establish similar institutions.

Nevertheless, the Marquis de Cavour, chief of the municipal police of Turin, again raised a formidable opposition, and he would doubtless have succeeded this time in having the Oratory closed if an unexpected protector had not arisen. The Count de Collegno, former Minister of State and Counsellor of Charles-Albert, declared that the king did not wish Don Bosco to be disturbed. The priest and the soldier, both men of action and devotion, always perfectly understood each other, and on more than one occasion the king testified his interest by gifts. Once especially, on the 1st of January, he sent three hundred francs with this superscription, "For Don Bosco's Little Rogues."

Some idea may be formed of the overwhelming labor accomplished by Don Bosco, when we consider that besides the great amount of time given to his Oratory he still managed to exercise his ministry in the prisons, the Cottolengo Hospital, at the Refuge, and also to visit the sick in the city. Moreover, he wrote for his children several works, the principal of which are "Sacred History for the Use of the Schools;" "Youth Instructed," a valuable work, which has gone through more than eighty editions; "The Metric System of Decimals;" "The Seven Dolors of the Blessed Virgin;" "Devotion to the Angel Guardian;" "Exercises on the Mercy of God;" "History of Italy;" "Abridged Ecclesiastical History;" etc. As no constitution could endure such labors, complete exhaustion soon reduced him to a very alarming state, and he was obliged by the imperative commands of the physician to retire for some time into the country. Here he should have taken a perfect rest, but the frequent visits of his children, together with the pupils and Brothers, left him no repose. Moreover, he returned to the city Saturday evening to hear confessions, and to assist at the reunions at the Oratory on Sunday.

In July, 1846, when making one of these journeys from the country, he took a cold which resulted in a severe inflammation of the lungs, which his poor exhausted body was little able to sustain.

The danger increased so much that the physicians lost all hope.

One night, which threatened to be his last, the Abbé Borel said to him, "Don Bosco, ask Almighty God to cure you."

"No," he replied, "I must abandon myself to the will of God."

"But you cannot leave your children; I beg of you, in their name, to ask God to cure you."

Then the poor sufferer, to gratify his friend, murmured, "O Lord, if it is Thy good pleasure, grant that I be cured! *Non recuso laborem.*"

"Victory!" the good Abbé exclaimed, "now I am sure you will recover."

And the next morning Don Bosco was in fact convalescent.

The children's great love for their devoted benefactor showed itself in the heroic vows and promises which they offered for his recovery, many of them so severe that Don Bosco had to interpose his authority to lighten some of the self-imposed penances, and forbid the accomplishment of others.

This illness so reduced the poor priest, already so much exhausted, that he was forced to take three months to recuperate.

This time was spent in his native place, Murialdo de Castelnuovo, not far from Turin, where his family owned a small property called Les Becchi.

When his strength began to return, nothing could keep him from his children, and October found him once more in his beloved Valdoco.

Having no longer the use of the little apartment formerly allowed him by the

Marquise Barolo, he determined, in order to save time, to take up his abode at the Oratory, and for this object rented from Pinardi some small rooms quite near the chapel. Then needing some one to take charge of his household affairs, he took his mother to live with him.

Don Bosco preceded his mother in this work, but later she seemed in a measure to take precedence of her son, especially when he was ordained priest. Margaret Bosco venerated her son as much as she loved him, and instinctively understood the greatness of the work to which he devoted himself. She was a large-hearted, courageous woman, and relinquished without a moment's hesitation the home of her happy married life and the peaceful seclusion of Becchi, to share the labors of her son and devote herself to his adopted family.

On the 3d of November, 1846, the mother and son left Les Becchi on foot, with walking-sticks in their hands, one carrying a breviary under his arm, the other bearing a large basket of provisions. They had in their pockets all the money they possessed, and it did not weigh heavily. A short time before reaching their destination, while passing through Rondò, they met the Abbé Vola, who more than once had lent a helping hand to Don Bosco in the night-schools and in teaching the Catechism to the children.

"How tired you seem, my good friend! Where are you going?"

"My mother and I are going to establish ourselves at the Oratory."

"But you have neither position nor resources that I know of; how are you going to manage?"

"I know not, but Providence will provide."

Touched by so much faith and courage, the good Abbé handed his watch to Don Bosco, saying, "I have only my watch, but I wish you would take it as a foundation stone."

The next morning the watch was sold, for there was great need of even the simplest articles of furniture in this new household.

But there were other urgent expenditures. There was the rent, and numbers of children who had necessarily to be assisted. Some were out of employment, and would have starved but for the good bowl of soup given them by Madame Margaret Bosco; others were so miserably clad they had to be supplied with sufficient clothing to at least cover them.

Don Bosco then sold a small vineyard and a few acres of land, which comprised all his possessions. The mother disposed of her wedding presents. She had jealously preserved the beautiful linen and a few jewels received at her marriage, and valued them for their tender associations; but she unhesitatingly sold most of them, retaining a few to adorn the Blessed Virgin's altar.

Margaret Bosco soon attracted to her assistance several holy women, among them the excellent mother of the illustrious Archbishop of Turin. It is impossible to describe the devotedness of these indefatigable aids, whom the humblest and most tedious labor never wearied when there was question of the children.

In the beginning of the year 1847, Don Bosco, thus installed in the Oratory, set about improving the work, by giving it a more definite form, and by introducing more regularity in its minor details.

At this time he framed a *Rule*, a perfect model of its kind, which has since been adopted by many other schools besides the Salésian.

He instituted *officers*, selected from among the best, most intelligent, and above all the most pious of the children. Each officer had his particular duty as well as his share of supervision and responsibility, and great care was taken to train them, that they in their turn might train others.

The conduct to be observed in church, at class, and at recreation was minutely regulated; and in order to incite the children to greater piety Don Bosco established among them a *Society of St. Aloysius*, in which this Saint was held up as a model under all circumstances in life.

The worthy Archbishop of Turin, Monseigneur Franzoni, approved this Society; he moreover encouraged in every possible way all Don Bosco's efforts, and as a proof of his interest gave Confirmation to the children in the humble chapel of the Oratory of Valdoco.

This ceremony took place on the feast of SS. Peter and Paul, the 29th of June, 1847, and every effort was made to give it all the pomp and solemnity possible.

Flags covered all the defects in the walls of the chapel; flowers and plants, and a triumphal arch of branches erected in front of the entrance, completed the decorations. When the Bishop ascended the pulpit and attempted to remove his mitre the ceiling proved rather low, but that did not lessen the electrifying effect of the words he addressed to his young, enthusiastic audience.

These results did not suffice to satisfy the heart of the young priest who had become the tender, watchful father of his adopted family. He sighed to see many of his children, in consequence of their precarious position and the uncertainty of obtaining work, left without shelter, obliged to sleep in stables and sheds, and even in lodgings still more injurious to them. Nothing could be more fatal than the deplorable surroundings with which they were forcibly brought in contact. It is well known how impressionable youth is, and not a few children were thus lost. To obviate this evil, Don Bosco procured a hayloft in the neighborhood of the Oratory, had the floor covered with fresh straw, and with the aid of a few quilts afforded at least a temporary lodging to those children left in the streets. When the coverings failed he took bags. Those accustomed to sleep in the streets knew well how to appreciate these bags; they crept into them, and thus had linen under and over them.

This primitive dormitory rendered good service. But Don Bosco soon learned that letting furnished lodgings was not all rose-colored. While he received only the children who frequented the Oratory all went well; but one day, or rather one evening, his charity led him to offer hospitality to a troop of little vagabonds he met in the waste lands which then surrounded the Oratory. Hoping to do them some good, he offered to lodge them. But in the morning, when he went to give them a few words of good advice, he found the place empty, not a single coverlid remained, not even a bag: they had carried them all off.

This unlucky adventure, far from discouraging Don Bosco, only incited him to do still more. A short time after this, in the month of May, an orphan, guided no doubt by the Blessed Virgin, presented himself at Don Bosco's door. He was a mason's apprentice, who had come to Turin in search of work; the small amount of money which composed all his savings was long since expended, and he had yet found no employment.

The rain was falling in torrents this evening, and the poor child was wet from head to foot. Margaret Bosco soon made a bright fire to warm the guest whom Divine Providence had sent to her hearth. When she had given him his supper, she placed a straw pallet in the middle of the kitchen, with sheets and coverings, and on this princely bed the poor child slept more contentedly than a king. This was the first boarder at the Oratory; soon a second came, then a third; finally they increased to seven.

Then they had to stop: it was impossible to accommodate another child, so small were the lodgings occupied by Don Bosco and his mother.

They were no less crowded in the place used for the reunions of the children. They came in such numbers that on certain feast-days there assembled as many as eight hundred.

The chapel, which was much frequented by the neighbors, could not accommodate them in addition to the children, many of whom were obliged to remain during the services in the class-rooms or in the court.

There was the same difficulty at the recreations: the children were so crowded together their games became very difficult, sometimes impossible.

Some measures must be taken.

Don Bosco and the Rev. Abbé Borel, his faithful companion in all his labors, held counsel together, and decided without hesitation that the only means of obviating this difficulty was to establish a second Oratory, and the Archbishop's approval having been obtained, they set to work without delay.

They rented a convenient locality—the place where the court of Victor Emmanuel II. now stands. The beautiful streets, costly dwellings, and carefully kept gardens which now adorn this quarter did not then exist. There was nothing to be seen but a few small houses, and a few scattered, ruined hovels, occupied principally by washerwomen, attracted here by the nearness of the river Po.

The place selected was doubly favorable: they could do good to the population inhabiting that quarter, besides saving many of the children a long walk to and from their homes.

The new Oratory was called The Oratory of St. Louis, in honor of the venerable Archbishop of Turin, who bears that name, and also in compliment to the Society of St. Aloysius, recently established among the young men. A great many people of the world took great interest in this foundation, and aided it with their money or labor; so that the excellent society of coöperators worked admirably even from the beginning, before it was incorporated in the rules; thus giving evident proof of its usefulness. Nearly everything necessary to furnish the chapel was donated, and the ladies embroidered with their own hands the greater part of the linen and vestments.

The Oratory of St. Louis was solemnly opened on the 8th of December, 1847. A memorable anniversary; for on the 8th of December, 1841, Don Bosco received the first child of his adopted family. On the 8th of December, 1844, he inaugurated the Oratory of St. Francis de Sales in the house of the Marquise Barolo; and three years afterward, in 1847, he said Mass for the first time at the Oratory of St. Louis.

It can be seen how far the work had progressed in that comparatively short time. Two houses existed—very poor indeed in this world's goods, but most rich in the sight of God. Eight hundred children receiving the Word of God! What a marvellous treasure! The clergy of Turin, encouraged by their worthy Archbishop, earnestly lent their coöperation to the new Oratory. Several priests, under the eminent direction of the Rev. Abbé Borel, successively assumed the duties of director and chaplain, while others assisted in teaching. This state of things continued until the Oratory of St. Francis de Sales was able to furnish priests from among its members, who definitely undertook the direction of the house.

Meanwhile Don Bosco actively occupied himself with his Oratory of St. Francis de

Sales, still installed in the Pindari house and shed. His great desire was to furnish food and lodgings to a certain number of children, many of whom were beyond his influence, having no assured shelter, and being compelled to earn with difficulty their daily bread. They could not even come to the Oratory on Sunday, and his best efforts were rendered useless by their deplorable poverty.

To buy the Pinardi house was hardly possible. Eighty thousand francs was the price asked for it—a sum entirely beyond his slender resources. He had to content himself with renting successively all the rooms as they were vacated by the boarders, and he devised every means of using to the best advantage a place as insufficient as it was inconvenient.

The year 1848 was a very trying one. The people were agitated and misled by revolutionary doctrines. The children could not escape such an influence, and many of them were led away and disappeared, and others became less assiduous and docile.

Don Bosco had to be satisfied with redoubling his efforts and devotion. He well knew that nothing was more capable of attracting and keeping the young people than the care which he took to instruct them. He at once considerably enlarged the schools, and thus was able to receive in the night classes more than three hundred young men: a large number, when we consider how difficult it was to make them all study with profit.

At this time he established the custom, which has always been continued in the Salésian houses, of finishing the evening's work by giving a short instruction to the children. The simplest and also the most impressive truths were explained to them. The light of infinite love was made to shine upon their young souls, as the surest means of withdrawing them from the degrading influences of evil. This practice produced marvellous fruit. A great number of the children from that time really entered a life of perfection; many manifested sentiments of deep and solid piety, and many religious vocations were developed. By prodigious efforts Don Bosco succeeded in supplying fifteen boarders with food and lodging at the Oratory.

There were fifteen other children to whom he gave food only. These children went to their work in Turin and slept at home, but they came to the Oratory for their meals. And it may be readily imagined that Don Bosco did not fail to avail himself of these occasions to give them a few words of good advice. That a greater number might profit by this arrangement he received them by series; that is, fifteen children slept and took their meals in the house from Sunday morning till Saturday evening, then the next week fifteen others took their places.

This plan was most ingenious in the good which it effected. But it no doubt entailed an extraordinary amount of care, the burden of which fell upon Don Bosco and his mother.

While good Madame Margaret was busily at work in the kitchen, occupied with the household affairs, yet finding time also to mend the children's clothes, Don Bosco was often seen doing the heavy work of the house, drawing water, sweeping, sawing the wood, lighting the fire, shelling the peas and peeling the potatoes. He did not hesitate in case of necessity to don an apron and make the *polenta* himself, and on those days it was pronounced to be particularly good.

Cutting out and even sewing a pair of pantaloons were not beyond his skill, and the repairs which he sometimes made on the children's clothes made up in strength for what they lacked in artistic finish. As to the refectory, it was of the most primitive kind. Each one seated himself where and how he could: some in the court on a stone or block of wood, others on the steps of the stairs, and the bowls were emptied as if by magic.

A spring of fresh water flowed near by, furnishing a drink as healthy as it was abundant. When the repast was finished, each one washed his bowl and put it away in a safe place. As to the spoons, being very precious objects, and having no drawer in which to keep them, each one kept his in his pocket. What honest sweet happiness was enjoyed in this poor household, small court and humble rooms! After grace, Don Bosco was accustomed to say to his guests, "Good appetite," and this innocent recommendation was invariably greeted with a great burst of laughter.

The good father possessed an inexhaustible fund of gayety and youthful spirits; no one knew better than he how to amuse and interest the children. He told a story with charming humor, mingled with remarkable delicacy and grace of expression. What was wanting to the repasts in the way of seasoning was more than made up by the hearty appetites and joyousness of the guests.

Don Bosco's table was no better supplied than the children's: bread and soup, soup and bread, this was the usual bill of fare for everybody.

More than once ecclesiastics who came to assist him were obliged to leave, not being able to endure such very primitive fare. Besides the time devoted to his dear Oratory, Don Bosco managed to give private lessons to poor young men in the city, in whom he recognized special talents or a dormant vocation.

His excellent method and inexhaustible patience soon produced most distinguished pupils. Nor did he neglect for this his visits to the prisons, the Cottolengo Hospital, and to the sick nor the confessions, etc.; and above all, he made every effort to enlarge and perfect the night-school, a work which supplied in a most special manner the needs of the time. He made the study of vocal and instrumental music a very important branch in the schools. The charming voices of some of the children and the perfection of their singing impressed the people, in whom a love of music is innate. This was an additional attraction, and the number of children in the school continued to increase. Numbers of young professors and organists were educated in these schools, and exhibited remarkable talent.

The study of music became a specialty in all the Salésian houses. As soon as a foundation was established a young organist was at once appointed, and he was generally one of the children who had shown musical ability, and who continued to perfect himself while giving lessons and playing the harmonium at the church services.

Music is a specific means of moral and intellectual culture and a great aid in all religious services. The success of the night-schools was so well appreciated, that the Municipality of Turin gave Don Bosco a prize of six thousand francs in recognition of his services, and later a prize of a thousand francs for music, to which was added an annual subsidy, which was paid until 1872.

The pastors of Turin objected to the functions of the parish, first Communion, Confirmation, etc., being performed in a private institution, and complained to the Bishop; but as he had always cordially supported Don Bosco, he now invested him with the full powers of a parish priest, and the Oratory became *The parish of neglected children*.

It is incomprehensible that this poor priest, so devoted to his apostolic mission, should be pursued by secret animosity. This was a point of resemblance between him and St. Francis de Sales. The numerous attempts made to assassinate Don Bosco can only be attributed to the diabolical influence which then prevailed. We shall see later in what miraculous ways he escaped the attacks of those who attempted his life.

In 1849 his trials were not lessened. The spirit of revolt still spread its evil counsels, but this was all the more reason for making greater efforts to counteract it. In that year Don Bosco founded at Turin a third Oratory. It was established in the Vanchiglia quarter, then extremely poor, and entirely without a church. This Oratory was called the Angel Guardian. Later the Church of St. Julia was built near it, by the generosity of the Marquise Julia Barolo, and it was formed into a parish, to which all this quarter now belongs.

The exigencies of the war, then being waged with Austria obliged the government to quarter the soldiers in the different seminaries, from which the students were in consequence expelled. Don Bosco readily received as many as he could accommodate, and the Oratory for a time was a sort of branch of the diocesan seminary. He lodged and fed thirty of the seminarians. Don Bosco's joy was very great at this time, for four of his children from the Oratory were invested with the *soutane* in October, 1849. These were the first scholastics from this Institution of St. Francis de Sales, which was to assume such gigantic proportions.

Since 1846 Don Bosco had rented first a part and later the whole of Pinardi's house. In the beginning of the year 1851 he became most unexpectedly its proprietor.

Pinardi had always said that he would never part with his real estate for less than the exorbitant sum of eighty thousand francs. One day accosting Don Bosco in a tone of half jest, he said,

"Well, Don Bosco does not care to buy my house?"

"Don Bosco will buy it when Mr. Pinardi will give it to him for a reasonable price."

"I ask eighty thousand."

"Then let us say no more about it."

"What do you offer then?"

"This building is valued at twenty-six or twenty-eight thousand francs: I will give you thirty for it."

"Will you add five hundred as pin-money for my wife?"

"I will make that present."

"You will pay the money down?"

"I will pay the money down."

"In one payment, and in fifteen days?"

"As you wish."

"A hundred thousand francs forfeiture?"

"Well, a forfeiture of a hundred thousand francs."

They shook hands, and the bargain, which had hardly taken five minutes, was concluded. As usual, Don Bosco had not the first cent of this sum; but there was question of the welfare of his children, so he had absolute confidence. Scarcely had Pinardi taken his departure when the Abbé Cafasso entered, bringing ten thousand francs—a generous gift from the Countess Casazza Ricardi.

The next morning a Rosminian Father came to the Oratory to consult Don Bosco about investing the sum of twenty thousand, which had been entrusted to his care. Here was a splendid opportunity. The banker Cotta added three thousand francs, and this large amount was thus secured.

The Pinardi house was bought and paid for February 19th, 1857, and Don Bosco at once set about building a church in honor of St. Francis de Sales. The one he had improvised was in a basement and consequently damp; besides which, there was so little ventilation, that often during the services the children became faint, and almost smothered for want of air.

The plan was drawn by the ingenious Blachier, and the foundation was begun at once. There was the usual absence of resources, and the usual visible intervention of Divine Providence.

An unexpected subsidy from Victor Emmanuel, numerous offerings, and finally a lottery, furnished the necessary funds.

On the 20th of January, 1852, the Church of St. Francis de Sales was solemnly consecrated. The members of the Oratory then recalled certain certain words of Don Bosco, which had passed unnoticed at the time, but with the realization of which they were now impressed.

In 1846, when they lowered the ground under the shed to transform it into a chapel, the children during recreation amused themselves by climbing on the mounds of earth which had been dug out.

One Sunday Don Bosco climbed one of the mounds with them, and made them sing several times to a particular air the following stanza:

> Praised be forever
> The names of Jesus and Mary;
> Forever praised be
> The name of Jesus incarnate.

Then he said, "My children, some day, on this very spot where we now stand, the altar of a beautiful church will be raised, and you will come and kneel here to receive Holy Communion, and sing the praises of God."

Five years afterward the Church of St. Francis de Sales covered this site, and the altar occupied the exact spot indicated by Don Bosco.

Having built a temple to God, Don Bosco turned his attention to a house for his children. It was necessary to give them a permanent home in order to shelter them from the temptations of the street.

He went at once to work, and large buildings rose in succession around the chapel. But this Oratory of St. Francis de Sales, which was to be the asylum of so many innocent souls, thirsting for perfection and even for sanctity, was not achieved without enduring even severe material trials.

First, there was, on the 26th of April, 1852, a terrible explosion of a powder-mill situated about five hundred yards from the Oratory, which might have levelled it to the ground; stones weighing from two to three hundred pounds were thrown into the air, and enormous burning beams fell in the court. Many walls were cracked by the concussion, and it was astonishing that the church, which had only just been finished, should have remained standing. The damage was repaired, and as soon as the church was consecrated, a large detached building, which was really indispensable, was begun.

This building was nearly finished, the beams of the roof were in place, and nothing was wanting but the tiles, when suddenly the rain came down in torrents. During the night between the 2d and 3d of December, the walls, loosened by the rain, fell with a frightful crash. Here, as at the time of the powder explosion, none of the household was injured.

The next morning the Inspector of Buildings sent an architect to examine the place. He noticed a large column, which, though out of plumb, yet supported a small house.

"Was this house occupied last night?" he asked.

"I slept there with thirty of the children."

"Well, Monsieur l'Abbé, you may thank Our Lady: this pillar stands contrary to all the laws of equilibrium, and it is a miracle that you were not all crushed to death."

The next year they were able to resume work on this building and complete it.

In 1860, when the Oratory was more severely menaced than ever, Don Bosco did not hesitate to purchase a large house, to which he added a story, thus doubling the accommodations for his orphans. Other buildings were added in 1862 and 1863. If the architecture of the Oratory of St. Francis de Sales of Valdoco as it now stands is somewhat irregular, it at least substantially realizes that famous plan, the description alone of which caused Don Bosco at one time to be considered insane. It can now accommodate a thousand people, besides the day pupils. It contains large workshops, where the children learn the different trades of carpenter, blacksmith, locksmith, tailor, shoemaker, baker, and bookbinder.

The printing establishment is very handsome, and beautifully fitted up. It has already furnished more than two hundred moral and educational works, as well as works of piety. A type-foundry, a shop for the manufacture of glazed paper, and another for photography and photo-engraving, complete the important trade of bookmaking. Finally, there is a large store, containing every variety of objects.

In 1865 Don Bosco laid the foundation-stone of a church dedicated to Our Lady Help of Christians, close by the Oratory.

This magnificent edifice was completed in 1868, and attracts great numbers of the faithful.

The Salésian work soon spread in a most astonishing manner. The advantages of these popular institutions, destined for the reception of poor neglected children, were so evident, that several other cities begged for Oratories like those of Turin.

Foundations of this kind were established at first in Italy, then in France, in Spain, and even in America.

There are in Italy, besides the three Oratories of Turin, and various smaller establishments, the Oratory and Hospital of St. Bénigne; the Collegiate Seminary of St. Charles, at Borgo San Martino; the College of St. Philip de Néri, at Lanzo-Torinese; that of the Immaculate Conception, at Valsalice, near Turin; of St. John the Baptist, at Varazze; of Our Lady of the Angels, at Alassio; the Manfredini House, at Este; the Hospital of St. Vincent de Paul, at San Pier d'Arena; the St. Paul Schools at La Spezia; the Oratory of the Cross, at Lucca; the Collegiate seminary of the Immaculate Conception, at Magliano Sabino; the establishment of St. Basile, at Randazzo; and of Bordighierra, the Parish and Hospital of the Sacred Heart at Rome.

There are four houses in France. The first one was established at Nice in 1875, and bears the name of the Patronage of St. Peter. Then two farm-houses—that of St. Joseph, for boys, at Navarre, near La Crau d'Hyères; and St. Isidore, for girls, at St. Cyr, in the Var.

In 1878 Don Bosco founded at Marseilles the Oratory of St. Leo, which has already received more than three hundred children.

A house was opened in Spain, at Utrera, near Séville, in 1881, and two others in 1882. These extraordinary fruits not satisfying the great charity of his apostolic heart, Don Bosco undertook to extend the work of the Catholic missions to South America.

Our Lord Jesus Christ was the first missionary sent by His Heavenly Father, and all His disciples have endeavored to continue the great mission of the redemption of the world confided to His Apostles.

Don Bosco resolved to carry the light of the Gospel to the wild, savage tribes of Patagonia.

All the missionaries who had attempted to penetrate into these distant countries had been killed, and, tradition adds, eaten. Such is said to have been the fate of the numerous Jesuit Fathers who courageously went to this inhospitable country, never to be seen again.

Every effort was vainly made to dissuade Don Bosco from such an undertaking, but, fortified by the encouragement and blessing of His Holiness Pius IX., he sent forth his missionaries.

On November 11, 1875, the first Salésian priests set sail, under the guidance of Don Cagliero, and landed at Buenos Ayres on the 14th of December.

The great gentleness and exquisite sweetness of St. Francis de Sales again triumphed over savage barbarism.

The missionaries established themselves on the confines of Patagonia, and immediately founded there a church and school.

They began by attracting to themselves the children, then a few savages, and in this way secured their first neophytes.

When it was thought advisable, they attempted an expedition into the interior of the country. They went by sea; but a violent storm overtook the ship, and, after having been tossed about for thirteen days on a stormy sea, the unfortunate missionaries found themselves just where they had started from—at the entrance of the harbor of Buenos Ayres, to which they were obliged to return.

Repulsed by the sea, they set out by land. I will not enumerate the stirring adventures of this expedition, accomplished in the midst of so many dangers. But success crowned their generous efforts. To the Salésian priests is due the honor of having planted the cross in these savage countries.

Great numbers were baptized, churches and schools were built, as well as houses for the reception of children. The glad tidings were proclaimed that the great command, *Ite et docete omnes gentes* ("Go, preach to all nations"), was fulfilled.

The Salésian missions of South America are not confined to Patagonia. Missions, and foundations have been established also in the Argentine Republic, Paraguay, La Plata, Uruguay, Las Pampas, and others are soon to be founded in Brazil.

The following are the names of the principal houses in the order in which they were established:

College of St. Nicholas, of Los Arroyos.
Hospital of Mercy, at Buenos Ayes.

St. Charles in Almagro, at Buenos Ayres.

Parish of Carmen, in Patagonia.

Parish of Mercy, at Viedma, in Patagonia.

Villa Colon, near Montevideo.

Charity College, at Montevideo.

Oratory of St. Vincent de Paul, in the parish of Our Lady of Peace.

Las Piedras, in the parish of St. Isidore, near Montevideo.

Paysandù, the parish of Our Lady of the Rosary.

There are besides, in Patagonia, several other stations regularly attended at stated intervals.

To sum up in large numbers:

More than a hundred thousand children have been received in the Salésian houses in Italy, France, Spain, and in South America; besides furnishing to the Church a formidable militia of more than six thousand priests. The Word of God is spread in distant countries. Thousands of savages baptized.

The Sisters of Our Lady Help of Christians teach the little Patagonian girls.

Such is the Salésian work.

When we consider all that Don Bosco has accomplished we are struck with astonishment at the magnitude of the result obtained in so short a time. The hand of God is really visible here directing the man, who is but his instrument; but what marvels shine out in this simple and perfect course, which consists in unreserved abandonment to Divine Providence, seeking no other aid or support than the maternal assistance of the Blessed Virgin!

Let it not be imagined that Don Bosco is daring or rash in his undertakings. He never began a foundation until circumstances made it absolutely necessary; but when this was evident, he never hesitated, but went promptly to work, undeterred by want of funds, losing no time in considerations or useless preliminaries.

We must, he used to say, begin by taking the affair on our shoulders, and as we progress we soon find that the burden settles down and finds its equilibrium.

Nevertheless he always proceeded cautiously, and was humbly content at first with the most modest lodgings for his priests and children, satisfied, when he could procure it, to give them, in the beginning, bread and soup. Later, everything was much more generously supplied.

When a foundation was decided upon, he sent a few of his priests, *sine sacculo et sine perâ* ("without sack or scrip"), just as Our Lord told His Apostles to go.

The first time I had the pleasure of meeting a Salésian priest I could not help asking him, "Father, how do you manage to feed all these children?"

I will never forget the surprised expression of his face, and the tone in which he said, raising his hand to heaven, "Divine Providence."

For him, charged with providing for all the wants of these children of God, there existed not a shadow of a doubt of the certain and active intervention of Divine Providence. All the priests of the Oratory of St. Francis de Sales are thoroughly imbued with this imperturbable faith.

Don Bosco never enlarged any of his houses unless it was absolutely necessary; that is, he always waited until there was no more room to receive the children before adding to the building. Then he set to work with great confidence, assured that the necessary funds would not be wanting, but would come in good time. The living stones, so to speak, always preceded the material ones.

Don Bosco undeniably possesses exceptional administrative ability. There is in him the making of a great minister. He keeps in mind the most minute details of each of his houses. He knows the character not only of all his priests, his clerks and his professors, but also his children, all the co-operators whom he has seen or heard of, and all the benefactors of the work. He never forgets even those he meets casually.

His memory is astonishing. It is told that at the seminary he never bought a treatise on theology. The instructions he received sufficed him, and he could repeat them word for word. Half an hour was the time allowed in the morning for dressing. He was always ready in ten minutes, and spent the rest of the time reading Rohrbacher's History, which he thus learned by heart. He could at any time, if a verse were cited to him, repeat entire pages of Dante or Virgil.

These wonderful gifts explain how, although a shepherd till his fifteenth year, he nevertheless was able to acquire such profound and solid learning.

It is incomprehensible how, with poor health, failing sight, and weak limbs, he can endure such great, incessant labor; for, besides the direction of his numerous houses, Don Bosco is always ready to listen to sufferers and console them, and the number of these is certainly very great. He receives at least two hundred letters a day, and everywhere he goes innumerable people flock to see him.

It is true he finds in his priests and in many of the laity admirable assistants, whose zeal and devotion are untiring.

Then he has made it an invariable rule to attend to his immediate duties well, with great care, and without precipitation.

Although he has naturally a quick temper, he has acquired such perfect self-control that nothing can disturb his unalterable peace and serenity.

He is easy of access, and when any one is admitted to his presence he always receives him as if he were some distinguished personage who honors him by his visit. Although people sometimes take advantage of this and make him lose his valuable time, yet he never appears to think them importunate or the visit too long, and seems to have really nothing else to do but listen to them.

Never hurrying through his duties in order to accomplish a great deal, is the great secret of his success; bearing always in mind the favorite expression of one of our greatest surgeons, Nélaton, who, when he undertook a difficult and delicate operation, would say to his assistants, "Above all, let us not hurry, for we have no time to lose."

Foolish worldlings, to whom time is money or pleasure, need to reflect upon the value this useless struggle after perishable things will one day have, when weighed in the Divine balance.

All the Salésian houses are regulated by a uniform system.

The professors, instructors, and the heads of the different departments are generally Salésians, priests, ecclesiastics, or laymen. Foreign aid is sometimes called in requisition, according to the needs of the establishment. The children learn trades and receive elementary instruction.

Those who show decided ability and special talent become students. They are taught Latin and all the studies required by the government, so that they can aspire to administrative and professional careers.

Finally, a goodly number in whom a religious vocation is decidedly manifest become priests.

Among these Don Bosco recruits the greater part of his staff, besides the priests he furnishes to the different dioceses.

Most of the parish priests of Italy, especially of Northern Italy, come from the Oratory; and the Salésian houses supply half, and sometimes three quarters, of the staff of the large seminaries of Piedmont and Lombardy.

Don Bosco's method of teaching is simple and most efficacious, and is now adopted by many colleges and educational houses. The classical books he has written are also perfect models. We have known young men twenty years old, scarcely knowing how to read and write, competent, after a few years' study under his system, to enter a large seminary and to become learned priests.

In regard to moral training, the children in the Salésian houses are governed by the preventive method; that is, every effort is made to prevent their committing faults, to avoid the necessity of punishing.

The priests educated in Don Bosco's schools excel in the application of this method; thoroughly impregnated with the pure spirit of St. Francis de Sales, they know that to love the children and win their love is the best method of governing them.

The secret of this method is comprised in the words of St. Paul: *Charitas benigna est, patiens est; omnia suffert, omnia sperat, omnia sustinet* ("Charity is kind, is patient; beareth all things, hopeth all things, endureth all things").

The teachers always endeavor to win the hearts of the pupils and make every effort to prevent the slightest distrust, and in their relations in which affection replaces constraint, a word, a simple glance, is sufficient reproof. Severe reprimands and punishments are unnecessary.

The Salésian houses are above all particularly distinguished for the path of Christian perfection in which the children are carefully trained, and the enormous good resulting therefrom. The children make their first Communion very young, according to the custom in the early Church. When children are intelligent and sufficiently instructed, it is not necessary to consider the age, but allow them to approach the Holy Table, that the King of Heaven may come and reign in their innocent hearts.

"Nearly all the children receive Communion every Sunday, a great many two or three times a week, and some of them every day. Frequent confession and Communion and daily Mass are the pillars which should support all education, if we wish to abolish threats and punishments."

The children are scarcely ever left alone. All the young ecclesiastics and priests, after presiding in the workshops and at the classes, remain with the children, joining most heartily in their games. "Do whatever you like," said St. Philip Neri, "I will be satisfied if you do not commit sin."

Formerly Don Bosco himself joined in the games with incredible zest. He loves children devotedly, and the dear little creatures fully return his love. They never meet him without kissing his hand with an affection and tenderness touching to behold.

At one time Don Bosco could not appear in the streets of Turin without attracting a following of children.

The manner in which the different workshops are regulated is simply marvellous. The principal trades taught are those of printer, bookbinder, tailor. shoemaker, carpenter, blacksmith, as well as farming.

Poor human nature rebels against the hard law of labor; but the soul, if not neglected, may find in it a profitable means of advancement.

Often during the day, and especially in the evening after work, a few words of spiritual comfort are addressed to the children. They are reminded how manual labor was honored and glorified by Our Lord Himself, who was during his mortal life a simple workman like them. They are told of this adorable model and of his Heavenly Father, by whom He was received on His triumphant entry into heaven after the sorrows and trials of His life on earth.

The Christian workshop is a veritable abode of profound peace and unalterable happiness when the work is properly considered, and not merely endured, but joyfully accepted and sanctified. Armed with solid piety, these young men can valiantly encounter the difficulties of life, and walk unflinchingly in the right path; and such is generally the result of the Salésian teachings. A goodly number of them have attained very honorable positions. Some have become good merchants and noted manufacturers. Others have raised themselves to the highest places in the government, the public schools, the magistracy, and the army. But whether fortune smiles upon them, or whether they remain in the humblest position, their love for the house in which they were educated never alters. If it is in their power, they never fail to return every year to make a retreat; and they always retain unbounded veneration and gratitude for Don Bosco and their former masters.

But the characteristic trait of the thousands of children educated in the Salésian houses must not be forgotten. Not one of them, since the first day of the foundation, has ever been arrested or condemned by the judiciary.

It is a well-known, undeniable fact, that the Salésian Society, by its care of poor, abandoned children, renders signal service to the country. Twenty-five thousand children leave these houses every year, and the same number is received, and all these young men become good, honest citizens, men of worth and merit; thus this work contributes in a great measure to the honor and prosperity of the nation.

Applications come from all parts and all countries to Don Bosco for Salésian Institutes; but unfortunately he is unable to satisfy all the demands, for want of sufficient funds and for lack of assistants.

I now come to a subject which it is necessary to treat with great delicacy. I wish to speak of the innumerable cures and the signal favors obtained by Don Bosco, in which the direct intervention of the Blessed

Virgin, under the title of "Our Lady Help of Christians," is readily recognized.

These favors were especially manifested at the time Don Bosco commenced the beautiful church dedicated under this title. A sudden cure was obtained at the end of a novena to Our Lady Help of Christians, and soon resulted in an immense concourse of people coming from great distances, soliciting cures and graces of all kinds.

Don Bosco simply advised all of them to make a novena to Our Lady Help of Christians, and to promise an offering for her church if their prayers were granted. The offerings which came from this source —that is, from favors obtained—were so numerous and so large, that they alone almost sufficed to cover the entire expense of building this magnificent edifice.

These favors have since multiplied beyond computation, so that it is almost impossible to enumerate them.

Does it not seem evident that Our Lady Help of Christians thus wishes to testify how pleasing to her is the care taken of so many neglected children, and that the Divine Mother wishes to procure in this way the material resources necessary to sustain the Salésian work?

The amount realized from the labor of the children in the various shops is not sufficient to aid materially in the work of the Society. Most of them are young and yet unskilled in the trades they are learning, and many of them are students. It is appalling to estimate the enormous sum required to carry on this work.

A hundred thousand children, most of whom have to be fed and clothed; a hundred and thirty houses, in which the daily expenditure is very great; then the missionaries to be sent to foreign countries and supported. And, in addition to this heavy burden, His Holiness Leo XIII. has lately entrusted to Don Bosco the finishing of the Church of the Sacred Heart, now being built at Castro Pretorio, on Mount Esquiline, in Rome. He has to obtain the sum necessary to finish this important edifice, to which is to be attached a Salésian institute capable of accommodating a large number of children of all nationalities.

The Salésian work having no other resource than that of voluntary contributions, Our Lady Help of Christians ceases not to manifest her power, and to bestow favors on those who remember Don Bosco's children.

Hence, if people are not prompted by motives of faith and charity to render assistance, they may contribute through interested motives, for the promise is infallible.

"*Centies tantum nunc, in tempore hoc . . . et in sæculo futuro vitam æternam*" (Mark x. 30). "An hundred times as much now in this time . . . and in the world to come life everlasting." Some obtain material prosperity, others receive favors of a much higher order, graces and cures, such as a loved one rescued from the grasp of death, an invalid restored to health. . . .

Sometimes the cure is immediate, but generally it does not take place immediately, the disease following its natural course.

Don Bosco, like the Curé of Ars, dreads notoriety. He usually says to those who apply to him for prayers, "You will come at such a time to return thanks to Our Lady Help of Christians," or, "We will pray for you."

To obtain a favor, Don Bosco generally advises a novena to Our Lady, composed of *Three Our Fathers, Hail Marys, Glory be to the Fathers, and the Hail Holy Queen.* He has a singular devotion to this last prayer, and he never fails to furnish the person with a medal of Our Lady Help of Christians. He advises some work of charity as thanksgiving for graces obtained, but leaves everybody perfectly free in this matter, and in his delicacy refrains from even suggesting one of his own houses as the object of charity, although it is especially to these establishments that Our Lady Help of Christians has shown her protection.

He has the children in all the houses pray for the benefactors, and when a particular favor is asked, these prayers never fail to reach heaven.

It would require a very large volume to contain the history of the precious graces thus obtained; moreover, the time to reveal them has not yet come.

It can at least be said that those persons who have sought to obtain the protection of Divine Providence in their temporal affairs, by giving a tenth of their income to the support of these poor, abandoned children cared for in the Salésian houses, have in almost every instance realized this blessing beyond their greatest hopes or expectation.

If I thought it prudent, I could add to this sketch very many interesting facts. I could, for example, tell how, when His Holiness Pius IX. took refuge at Gaeta, Don Bosco prophesied to him the events that would signalize his reign. I could also speak of the singular esteem and veneration that this great Pope had for Don Bosco, sentiments in which his successor, Leo XIII., also shares. But all this will be told later much better than I could do it.

The following are the four principal works founded by Don Bosco:

1. The Salésian Association, with its priests, laymen, and missionaries.

2. The Institute of the *Daughters of Marie Auxiliatrice.*

3. The Society of *Marie Auxiliatrice*, for helping young men studying for the priesthood.

4. Finally, the Co-operators of St. Francis de Sales, a pious Association, of which we will give some details.

THE CO-OPERATORS OF ST. FRANCIS DE SALES.

WHEN Don Bosco began in 1841 to gather together poor, abandoned children from the streets and lanes of Turin, Providence soon sent him assistants who associated themselves with him in this noble work.

Several priests and laymen came to his assistance in the care of the children. Some taught them catechism, and helped in the classes; others obtained for those out of place good Christian masters.

As these poor little people were generally in rags, pious ladies of rank, and of all classes in Turin, took upon themselves the task of mending their clothes and of making them new ones.

Such was the origin of the Co-operators of St. Francis de Sales. Their number now exceeds eighty thousand, ten thousand of which are in France.

The Association did so much good, that Don Bosco, wishing to give it permanent form, framed for it, in 1858, rules, which he perfected in 1864 and 1868.

These rules were several times submitted to His Holiness Pius IX., and were finally finished and definitely adopted in 1874.

This Association of Salésian Co-operators received from Pius IX., of immortal memory, the most marked encouragement.

He had his name inscribed at the head of the list of Co-operators, and established the Association in the Third Order.

He commanded the Congregation of Rites to grant to said Co-operators all the indulgences that may be gained by the Tertiaries of the most favored orders, especially the Tertiaries of St. Francis of Assisi.

The following is the brief of Pius IX., dated May 9th, 1876.

" A pious Association of the faithful being canonically established, under the name of the *Society or Union of Salésian Co-operators*, the members of which propose, besides the exercise of different works of piety and charity, to take especial care of poor, abandoned children, in order to promote the daily increase of this Association, We, confiding in the mercy of Almighty God, and in virtue of the authority given His blessed

Apostles Peter and Paul, grant to all the faithful of both sexes, who belong and will belong in the future to this Society, a *plenary indulgence* at the hour of death, provided sincere repentance for sin is joined to the reception of the sacraments of Penance and the Eucharist, or if prevented from receiving them, they, with sincere contrition, devoutly invoke the name of Jesus at least in their hearts, and they accept death from the hand of God in a spirit of penance, and as a just chastisement for their sins. We likewise grant in the mercy of God another *plenary indulgence*, and the remission of all their sins, to those associates (which indulgence may be gained once a month on any day they choose) who, sincerely repentant, confess their sins and receive Holy Communion in some church or public oratory, and who afterward, devoutly visiting this same church or oratory, pray fervently to God for unity among Christian princes, for the extirpation of heresies, the conversion of sinners, and for the glory of our Holy Mother the Church. This indulgence is also applicable to the souls of the faithful who departed this life in union with God in the bonds of charity. Wishing, moreover, to give to the aforesaid associates a special mark of Our protection, We grant them, in virtue of Our apostolic authority, all the indulgences, plenary as well as partial, that may be gained by the Tertiaries of St. Francis of Assisi, and the privilege of lawfully and freely gaining on the feasts of St. Francis de Sales and in the churches of the Salésian priests all the indulgences granted the Tertiaries on the feast of St. Francis of Assisi, provided they faithfully fulfil in the name of God the works of piety enjoined for the gaining of these indulgences. And notwithstanding all else to the contrary, this present brief shall henceforth remain in force in perpetuity."

As soon as Leo XIII. was raised to the chair of Peter, he immediately wished to become, like Pius IX., a *Salésian Co-operator.* " Being inscribed as Co-operator," said he, " I wish to be the first operator;" and he has never failed to encourage and bless the work.

Here again are the exact words of Leo XIII. to Don Bosco: "Whenever you address the Salésian Co-operators, say that I bless them with all my heart; that the object of the Society is to prevent the ruin of youth, and that they should form one heart and one soul to aid in attaining the end proposed by this Association of St. Francis de Sales."

And as a proof of the importance he attaches to this work and of the interest he takes in it, our Holy Father Pope Leo XIII. has deigned to appoint the most eminent Cardinal, Lorenzo Nina, protector of the Salésian Society.

This Association thus markedly approved by the Church is a veritable Third Order, and may become the centre of all good works. The beautiful harvest of the Lord is ready; let the reapers hasten to the work.

Fides sine operibus mortua est (St. James). "Faith without works is dead."

Any one from the age of thirteen may become a Co-operator, and at his request a certificate of admission from an authorized Salésian priest will be sent to him. If the Co-operators observe the rules of the Association, they share, from the time of their admission, in all the favors, indulgences, and spiritual graces granted to the Society. They have part in all the Masses, prayers, novenas, missions, etc., and in all the works of charity performed by all the Salésians throughout the world. No pious practices are required of the Salésian Co-operators, except an *Our Father* and *Hail Mary*, once a day, in honor of St. Francis de Sales for the intention of the Holy Father. But the members are recommended to approach frequently the Sacraments of Penance and the Eucharist, and to make, if possible, a short retreat every year, and to perform every month the exercise for a happy death. Modesty in dress, sobriety, simplicity in their surroundings, fidelity to the duties of their state of life, seeing that those under their charge are faithful in the exact observance of Sundays and feast-days, are also recommended. The members of the Salésian Society regard all the Co-operators as brothers in Jesus Christ, and appeal to them whenever their concurrence may tend to the glory of God or the good of souls. The Co-operators, when necessary, apply with the same freedom to the members of the Salésian Society, for example, in case of sickness, or to obtain some grace. Special prayers are also offered for them after death.

The Co-operators should do all in their power to promote religious worship, endeavor to encourage religious vocations spread good books, and exercise their charity towards the poor abandoned children, whose salvation is endangered by their poverty.

They will, of course, make every effort to aid the Salésian works, either by making once a month, or at least once a year, an offering according to their means, or by collecting donations and alms by whatever means their charitable hearts may suggest.

We cannot do better than to give in conclusion a few words of Don Bosco's, addressed in a recent Salésian Bulletin *to his dear Co-operators:* "In the name of heaven, which is to be one day your recompense; in the name of the poor little creatures, who cannot plead for themselves; in the name of God, who promises an eternity of happiness to those who comfort the suffering—do not forget the work we have undertaken; never lose sight of your young protégés. If you have done all in your power for them, even if you have exceeded the limits permitted by your income, it still remains for you to recommend the work to your friends, procure for us new Co-operators, by making known the good that will accrue to themselves and to society. Form a sort of league to arrest the progress of demagogues, of immorality, and of the frightful scandals of the dissolute youth, who are making rapid strides towards atheism. And when you have done all that the love of religion inspires great souls to do, be assured that there still remains much good to be accomplished."

Dum tempus habemus operemur bonum. "Let us do good while we yet have time."*

DEVOTION TO OUR LADY HELP OF CHRISTIANS.

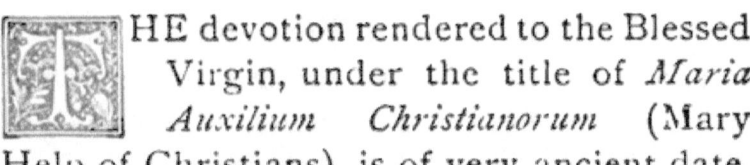HE devotion rendered to the Blessed Virgin, under the title of *Maria Auxilium Christianorum* (Mary Help of Christians), is of very ancient date.

---

* For the better understanding of this subject we should read a little pamphlet, to be had in all the Salésian houses, entitled "Salésian Co-operators, or practical means of aiding the Society for promoting good morals."

It also contains a complete list of all the indulgences that may be gained, as well as a short rule of life for the Salésian Co-operators.

But it was after the battle of Lepanto, in 1571, that it received in a manner official recognition.

The Christian fleet put to flight the Turkish fleet, to the cry of *"Live Mary;"* and Pope Pius V., learning by revelation this signal victory before the arrival of any messenger, commanded that the invocation *Mary Help of Christians, pray for us*, should hereafter be inserted in the Litany of Loretto.

A century later, in 1683, two hundred thousand Turks laid siege to the city of Vienna. Prince Charles of Lorraine had but thirty thousand men to oppose this invasion. Again the Pope, Innocent XI., came to the aid of the Christians, by ordering public prayers and by calling Christian princes to the assistance of the besieged city. Only one of them responded to the appeal—John Sobieski, of glorious memory. With a handful of men he entered Vienna, then a heap of ruins. On the 12th of September he went with Prince Charles to assist at Mass, which he himself served, kneeling with arms crossed; then he cried out, "Let us go forth under the protection of the Blessed Virgin to meet the enemy, and victory will be ours."

In fact, after a short battle the Turks retreated in confusion across the Danube, abandoning immense spoils. All Christendom unanimously attributed to the protection of the Blessed Virgin the astonishing victory which delivered not only Austria but Europe from the invasion of the Turks. On this occasion the first Confraternity in honor of *Mary Help of Christians* was established at Munich, in Bavaria.

Pius V. inserted in the Litany the invocation *Mary Help of Christians*, and Pius VII. instituted this feast on the 24th of May.

Exiled to Fontainebleau by Napoleon I., Pius VII. promised to honor the Blessed Virgin under the title of *Help of Christians*, if she would regain for him possession of the papal city.

On the 24th of May, 1814, he made his triumphal entry into Rome, and decreed that this date should be the feast of *Mary Help of Christians*.

In 1817, a painting, representing the Blessed Virgin under this title, was placed in the Church of *Santa Maria in Monticelli* at Rome. Numerous indulgences were granted to the Associations and Confraternity established in her honor; the faithful flocked here in great numbers, and signal graces were obtained.

The City of Turin was not backward in this devotion. It was the first to associate itself with the Confraternity of Munich, and it soon established a special Confraternity of *Our Lady Help of Christians,* which Pius VI., by a rescript dated February 9th, 1798, enriched with precious Indulgences and spiritual favors. This Confraternity held its meetings in the Church of St. Francis of Paul, where Cardinal Maurice, Prince of Savoy, who died in 1657, had a beautiful marble statue of Our Lady Help of Christians placed.

To extend this devotion to Mary Help of Christians, so popular in Turin, Don Bosco determined to erect in her honor a beautiful church at Valdoco.

This quarter, containing thirty-five thousand souls, was at that time entirely without a church. The little chapels of *La Providence* and the Oratory of St. Francis de Sales were absolutely insufficient for the accommodation of the faithful on feast-days, and even on Sundays.

If, heretofore, any doubt had existed with

regard to the advisability of this undertaking, it was removed by the august Pius IX., who, upon being informed of this design, immediately replied that the title of *Mary Help of Christians* would assuredly attract favors from the Queen of Heaven. He sent an offering of five hundred francs to help in the building of the church, and accompanied the gift with his special blessing.

Encouraged by this approbation, Don Bosco chose a suitable site very near the Oratory. Then the architect, Spezzia, drew a plan for a church in the form of a Latin cross, which was to cover a space of twelve hundred square metres.

The corner-stone was solemnly laid on the 27th of April, 1865.

When the work began there were but eight sous in the treasury, the five hundred francs sent by the Holy Father having been expended for the land.

Various sums had been promised by the municipality and by charitable persons, but for some unknown reason these promises were not very promptly fulfilled.

It was doubtless because of this failure of human aid that the intervention of the Queen of Heaven was manifested in so striking a manner, and that she thus clearly demonstrated her desire to have, not only an ideal temple in their hearts, but likewise a real edifice where her Divine Son would be honored through her mediation.

Undeterred by these difficulties, Don Bosco resolutely set the laborers to work digging the foundation.

In a fortnight the sum due to the workmen amounted to a thousand francs. These poor men could not wait any longer; they must absolutely be paid their wages. In this dilemma Don Bosco thought of a person who had begun a novena a few days before, and who had promised an offering if her prayers were answered.

This was a lady whom he had occasion to visit in the exercise of his holy ministry. She was very seriously ill, having been confined to her bed for three months with constant fever, and was completely exhausted by a severe cough.

"Oh! to recover my health a little," she had said to him, "I am willing to say all the prayers suggested to me, and to make an offering. I would consider it a great blessing if I were only able to leave my bed and walk a little about my room."

"Will you do what I suggest to you?"

"Most certainly."

"Then begin at once a novena to *Our Lady Help of Christians.*"

"How shall I make it?"

"For nine days say three times a day an *Our Father*, a *Hail Mary*, *Glory be to the Father*, and *Hail Holy Queen.*"

"I will do it; and what work of charity shall I add to it?"

"If you experience any improvement in your health, you may, if you wish, make an offering to the Church of Our Lady Help of Christians, which has been begun at Valdoco."

"Yes, yes, very willingly; if during this novena I only obtain strength enough to leave my bed and walk a little in my room, I will make an offering to the church that is being built in honor of the Blessed Virgin Mary."

This promise was Don Bosco's sole resource at this time.

This was just the eighth day of the novena, and it was not without a certain anxiety that he went to inquire the result of it.

The servant who opened the door exclaimed, as soon as she saw him, "Madame is cured! She has already been twice to the church to return thanks to God."

Her mistress then came forward, and, overcome with joy, said, "I am cured, Father; I have already been to thank the Blessed Virgin. Here is the offering I promised; it is the first, but it certainly shall not be the last;" and she handed Don Bosco a small package.

When he reached home he opened it and found exactly fifty gold Napoleons.*

The thousand francs, of which he had such need that day, may be said to have really fallen from the hands of the Blessed Virgin.

Although Don Bosco carefully avoided speaking of this affair, it was soon noised abroad and spread like an electric spark, and an extraordinary number of persons at once made novenas to *Our Lady Help of Christians*, promising offerings to her church if their prayers were heard.

It would be difficult to relate the many cures which were effected, and the graces of all kinds, spiritual and temporal, obtained. Turin, Genoa, Bologne, Naples, Milan, Flor-

---

* A Napoleon is twenty francs, or $3.87.

ence, Rome, as well as Palermo, Vienna, Paris, London, and Berlin, re-echoed the praises of *Our Lady Help of Christians*. No one ever had recourse in vain to her intercession.

The offerings came in great numbers, meeting every need. When the work was being pushed forward with the greatest activity the offerings seemed for a time to fall off. But suddenly the cholera appeared; many hearts were moved, some through fear of the scourge, others through gratitude for having escaped it, and the offerings became more abundant than ever. There were those who wished the protection of *Our Lady Help of Christians* either in their business or for the success of their crops, promising to give to the church a tenth of the profits of their harvest. They had no reason to regret this agreement, for the results surpassed all their expectations.

It is almost incredible that the Church of *Our Lady Help of Christians* was built without a single collection having been made; the funds always came of themselves, and just in time. The total expenditure amounted to a little over a million, and an exact account which was kept of all the money received, shows that of this immense sum eight hundred and fifty thousand francs were offerings made by persons in grateful acknowledgment of graces and special favors obtained. It may be said each stone in the edifice represented the goodness and power of *Mary Help of Christians.*

Long, indeed, would be the list if all the grateful offerings made to the church were enumerated; such as chalices, ciboriums, ostensoriums, lamps, valuable ornaments, altars, chandeliers, statues, paintings, etc.

The new temple, begun in 1865, was completed in three years, and was consecrated June 9th, 1868.

The celebration of this event lasted eight days, and attracted immense crowds of people. The august Pius IX. was pleased to grant a plenary indulgence, applicable to the souls in Purgatory, to all who, having confessed and received Holy Communion, made a visit to the Church of *Mary Help of Christians* during the first eight days after its consecration. The crowd was so great that it was impossible to enter or leave the church during the ceremonies, yet there was no confusion nor any accident.

The celebration was concluded by a requiem mass offered for the souls of all the deceased benefactors.

We shall not give a detailed description of this church, but will merely observe, that although it has only been open twelve years, the walls are already covered with a great number of votive offerings, undeniable testimonials of graces unceasingly obtained through devotion to *Our Lady Help of Christians.*

A CURE.

ARON COMMANDER COTTA, a banker and State Senator of Turin, was lying on his death-bed when Don Bosco came to see him.

"Father," said the sick man, in a voice so feeble it could scarcely be heard, "this is the last time I will ever see you; this is the end; I will not last through the day."

"Oh no, Commander! you will not go like that. The Blessed Virgin still has need of you in this world; you are too necessary to her in building her church."

"I would very much like to do something more, but the doctors say there is no hope."

"What will you do if *Our Lady Help of Christians* cures you?"

"If I get well, I will give to her church two thousand francs a month for six months."

"Very well, I will return to the Oratory and have everybody there pray for you. Have courage."

Three days afterwards Don Bosco was in his room when a visitor was announced. It was Baron Cotta, perfectly cured, who had come to make his first offering to *Our Lady Help of Christians*, and he has since made very many others to her church.

A MEDAL OF OUR LADY HELP OF CHRISTIANS.

ONE Saturday in the month of May, 1869, a young girl, her eyes covered with a thick black bandage, and led by two women, entered the Church of *Our Lady Help of Christians* at Turin. Her name was Mary Stardero, of the village of Vinovo, and for two years she had a severe inflammation of the eyes, which resulted in the loss of her sight.

She could not walk without a guide, so her aunt and a neighbor accompanied her on the pilgrimage she desired to undertake. Having prayed at the altar of the Blessed Virgin, she asked to speak to Don Bosco, and the following conversation took place in the sacristy:

"How long have your eyes troubled you?"

"I have suffered a long time with my eyes, but for nearly a year I have not been able to see."

"Have you consulted the doctors? What do they say? Have you used remedies?"

"We have," replied the aunt, "used all kinds of remedies, but none of them produce the slightest effect. The doctors say that the eyes are destroyed, and they give no hope;" then she began to cry.

"Can you distinguish large objects from small?"

"I cannot distinguish anything," she replied.

"Take off the bandage," said Don Bosco. Then, making the young girl face a very bright window, he said, "Do you see the light from this window?"

"Unfortunately for me I see nothing whatever."

"Would you like to see?"

"Can you ask! I wish it more than anything else in the world. I am a poor young girl, and the loss of my sight condemns me to a life of misery."

"You will use your eyes for the good of your soul, and not to offend God?"

"I promise that with all my heart;" adding with a sob, "mine is a very hard lot."

"Have confidence in the Blessed Virgin; she will help you."

"I hope so; but meanwhile I am blind."

"You will see."

"What! shall I see?"

"For the glory of God and the honor of the Blessed Virgin, name the object I hold in my hand?"

The young girl strained her eyes, and staring at the object, she cried out, "I see."

"What?"

"A medal."

"Of whom!"

"Of the Blessed Virgin."

"And what is on this side of the medal!"

"On this side, an aged man with a staff in blossom in his hand: it is St. Joseph."

"Holy Mother!" exclaimed the aunt, "you see, then?"

"Yes, I see, thanks be to God; the Blessed Virgin has obtained this favor for me."

At that moment she put out her hand to take the medal, but it fell and rolled into a dark corner of the sacristy.

The aunt bent down to pick it up, but Don Bosco held her back. "Let her do it; we will see if the Blessed Virgin has perfectly restored her sight."

The young girl immediately found the medal without the least difficulty. The poor girl was so beside herself with happiness that she left the church without a word of thanks to Don Bosco, or even to God, and eagerly ran towards Vinovo, uttering wild cries of joy, accompanied by her aunt and the neighbor.

She returned later, however, to give thanks to the Blessed Virgin, and did not forget to make an offering for her church. Since then her eyes have never troubled her, and she leads a perfect life.

A singular fact in connection with this is,

that the aunt who accompanied her was at the same time cured of violent rheumatic pains she had had for a long time in her shoulder and arm, and which prevented her from working in the fields.

THE INCREDULOUS PHYSICIAN.

 PHYSICIAN highly esteemed in his profession, came one day to the Oratory of St. Francis de Sales and asked to see Don Bosco, whom he thus addressed:

"It is said that you cure all kinds of diseases."

"I? Not at all."

"They have assured me of it, giving the names of the persons and the nature of the disease."

"Many persons come here to ask graces through the intercession of *Our Lady Help of Christians*. If, after a triduum or novena, they happen to be cured, I have nothing to do with it. This favor is entirely due to the Blessed Virgin."

"Very well. Let her cure me also, and I will believe in these miracles."

"What is your malady?"

"I have had epileptic fits, and in the last year the attacks have become so severe that I cannot go out alone for fear of accident. Nothing gives me any relief, and in despair I have come here, like so many others, to seek a cure."

"Then do as the others do. Kneel down and say some prayers with me; prepare yourself to purify and strengthen your soul by confession and Communion, and the Blessed Virgin will console you."

"Order me to do something else, for that I cannot do."

"And why?"

"It would be hypocrisy on my part. I believe neither in God nor the Blessed Virgin, nor in prayers nor miracles."

Don Bosco was at first amazed; but, aided by the Holy Spirit, his words touched the doctor's heart, and he knelt and made the sign of the cross.

"I am surprised that I still know how to do this, for it is forty years since I have done anything of the kind."

He said the prayers, and then made his confession. Immediately afterward he felt inwardly convinced that he was cured. He has never had the slightest return of the attacks, and he comes often to return thanks to *Our Lady Help of Christians*, who cured his body and his soul.

THE GOLD BRACELET.

ON the feast of *Mary Help of Christians*, the 24th of May, 1878, a young officer came to the Oratory of St. Francis de Sales at Turin, whose countenance expressed suffering, and whose voice shook with emotion.

"Father," said he to Don Bosco, "my wife was some time ago attacked with a severe illness, and it is feared that she will die. I cannot be resigned to the thought of losing her; I beg of you to obtain from God the favor of her cure."

Don Bosco consoled and comforted him; then, seeing him well disposed, he took advantage of it to make him kneel and say with him some prayers for the health of his sick wife. The officer had scarcely been gone an hour when he was seen returning in great haste.

"I wish to speak to Don Bosco."

"It is impossible just now; he is presiding at a meeting of the Benefactors of the house, who are assembled on the occasion of this solemn feast, and we cannot disturb him."

"Tell him my name, and that it is absolutely necessary for me to see him a moment."

Thus importuned, Don Bosco came to see the officer, whose face now beamed with joy.

"Do you know, Father, that while I was with you, my wife, whom I left on her death-bed, felt her sufferings cease and her strength return; she asked for her clothing; and oh, what a miracle!—when I entered the house she came to meet me, saying she was cured."

Then taking from his pocket a gold bracelet he gave it to Don Bosco.

"This is a present I gave my wife when we were married; we both offer it with all our hearts to *Our Lady Help of Christians*, in gratitude for such an un-hoped-for cure."

Don Bosco returned to the meeting of Benefactors and showed them the bracelet. "This," said he, "is an offering in gratitude for a new cure which has just been obtained through the intercession of *Mary Help of Christians.* Praise be to her name!"

MIRACULOUS CURE OF A SICK MAN.

ON the evening of the 16th of November, 1866, while the Church of *Our Lady Help of Christians* was being built, Don Bosco had to pay the men at work on the cupola four thousand francs, and he did not have the first cent of this sum. From early morning Don Rua, prefect of the house, and several assistants had been out trying to collect the amount. Innumerable were the streets they traversed and the stairs they mounted, and at eleven o'clock they returned with a thousand francs, which was all they could possibly obtain.

As they stood silently looking at each other in consternation, Don Bosco began to laugh, and said, "Very well, I will go after dinner and look for the rest."

At one, he took his hat and went out, trusting that something providential would occur. After taking several turns at random he came to the *Porte-Neuve*; there he stopped to decide which way he should direct his steps. At that moment he was accosted by a servant in livery.

"Monsieur l'Abbé, are you not Don Bosco!"

"Yes; what can I do for you?"

"My master sent me to beg you to come to him at once."

"Let us go to your master: is it far?"

"No: he lives there at the end of the street;" and he pointed out a magnificent house.

"That house belongs to him?"

"Yes, and he is immensely wealthy, and could easily afford to do something for your church."

On arriving, the Abbé was ushered into

a beautiful room, where, extended on a bed, lay a middle-aged man, who expressed great joy on seeing Don Bosco.

"Reverend Father, I have great need of your prayers; you must put me on my feet again."

"Have you been ill long?"

"I have not left this bed of suffering for three years; I am perfectly helpless; and the doctors give me no hope. If I obtain the slightest relief, I will willingly make an offering for your good works."

"This happens most opportunely: we have need this very day of three thousand francs for the Church of *Our Lady Help of Christians.*"

"Three thousand francs! You do not appreciate what an amount you ask for. If it were a few hundred francs, I might consider it; . . . . but three thousand francs!"

"Is it too much?" asked Don Bosco; "then let us say no more about it."

Then, seating himself, he began quietly to discuss the politics of the day.

"But, Father, that is not the subject in question; what about my cure?"

"Your cure! I suggested a means, but you could not do it."

"But you also asked three thousand francs."

"I do not insist upon it."

And he began to talk of indifferent things.

"Obtain me a little respite from my suffering, and I certainly will not forget you at the end of the year."

"At the end of the year! You do not understand, then, that we need the money this very day."

"This very day! You must know that I have not three thousand francs in the house; it would necessitate sending to the bank, and that requires some effort on my part."

"Why not go to the bank?"

"You are jesting: that is impossible. I have not been able even to leave my bed for three years."

"Nothing is impossible to God, and *Mary Help of Christians*."

Saying this, Don Bosco assembled all the members of the household, to the number of thirty, and said with them a prayer to the

Blessed Sacrament and to *Our Lady Help of Christians.* Then he ordered the sick man's clothing to be brought.

"His clothing! but he has none; he has not been dressed for three years; we do not know where his clothes are."

"Let some be bought for me at the nearest shop," cried the sick man, with impatience; "do as the Father tells you."

During this scene the doctor entered and wished to prevent what he called an unheard-of piece of folly.

But when the clothes came, the sick man dressed himself, and took long strides across the room, to the inexpressible astonishment of all present.

He ordered the carriage, and while waiting regaled himself with a lunch, which he ate with an appetite long denied him.

Then, in the full vigor of health, he descended the stairs unaided, and stepped into the carriage.

A few moments afterward he brought to Don Bosco three thousand francs.

He kept constantly repeating "I am perfectly cured."

"You brought the money out of the

bank," said Don Bosco, "and *Our Lady Help of Christians* brought you out of your bed."

This man has continued a faithful benefactor of the work, and he has contributed liberally to the building of the Church of *Our Lady Help of Christians*.

CURE OF A GENERAL.

 GENERAL residing at Turin became seriously ill, and was soon reduced to the last extremity. He made his confession to Don Bosco, but he, to the surprise of all the family, did not give the sick man Communion, although the physicians said he was in imminent danger.

It was the 22d of May. "General," said Don Bosco, "the day after to-morrow we shall celebrate the feast of *Our Lady Help of Christians;* pray fervently to her, and on that day come and receive Holy Communion in her church, in thanksgiving for your cure."

On the 23d the General grew much worse; death seemed very near. The family, not wishing to let him leave this world without the strengthening grace of all the Sacraments, knew not what to do, for Don Bosco had told them he was not to receive Extreme Unction in his absence. A messenger was sent at eight in the evening to warn Don Bosco, of the sick man's great danger, and that it was feared he would not last through the night.

The day before a feast so dear to the Salésian family, Don Bosco was in the confessional from early morning, and when they came to look for him he was surrounded by numbers of children still waiting to be heard.

"Come quickly, Father," said the messenger; "the General is dying, and you will scarcely have time to get to him."

"But do you not see that I am hearing confessions; I cannot send these poor little things away. I will go as soon as I am through."

And he went on hearing the confessions.

It was eleven when he finished.

A carriage awaited him at the door.

"Make haste, I beg of you, Father."

"I will, but I have eaten nothing since morning and I feel quite exhausted; if I do not take my supper before midnight I will have to go without food, of which I feel great need; for to-morrow I have to be in the confessional from five in the morning."

"Do come now, Father; you will have some refreshment at the house."

He entered the carriage, and as soon as he reached the house they cried,

"Hurry, hurry, Father; we feared you would not be in time to administer the last Sacraments; the poor General is very low."

"O ye of little faith! Did I not tell you that the General would receive Communion to-morrow, the feast of *Mary Help of Christians?* It is almost twelve; have the goodness to give me some supper."

Don Bosco seated himself at table with that calmness which he always possessed, and when he had finished, he ordered the carriage and departed.

As to the General, he was supposed to be dead. He was perfectly motionless, and they knew not what to think of it. But he was simply sleeping.

The next morning at an early hour he asked his son to have his clothes brought to him, for he wanted to go and receive Communion from the hands of Don Bosco, as he had agreed to do.

About eight in the morning Don Bosco was in the sacristy vesting for Mass, when an emaciated figure entered.

"Here I am, Father."

"Very good, my dear sir; but excuse me if I ask to whom I have the honor of speaking."

"What! do you not recognize the General?"

"Ah! Praise be to *Our Lady Help of Christians*, I told you that you would come to her sanctuary on her feast-day."

"Father, will you be kind enough to hear my confession, for I would like to receive Communion at your Mass, as you told me to."

"But you went to confession the day before yesterday; that is sufficient."

"I would at least accuse myself of a want of faith, of which I now recognize myself guilty."

Don Bosco gave him absolution, and

Holy Communion, and the General returned home perfectly cured.

A CRIPPLE.

ON the feast of Corpus Christi, the 4th of June, 1874, when the sacristan was opening the Church of *Our Lady Help of Christians* at Turin, he found lying on the ground in front of the middle door a man who seemed to be ill.

When asked what he wanted, he said he had come to implore *Our Lady Help of Christians* to bless and cure him. He was conducted, or rather carried, to the sacristy; for although he used a strong crutch, he was obliged to lean heavily on the man who helped him, his limbs were so twisted and contracted; besides which, he was nearly bent in two.

The priests were busy in the confessionals, or saying their Masses. About eight Don Bosco entered the sacristy."

"What do you wish, my friend?"

"I ask *Mary Help of Christians* in charity to bless and cure me."

"What is your disease?"

"I am completely disabled with rheumatism, which has deprived me of the use of my limbs; the doctors call it a spinal affection."

"How were you able to get here?"

"Last night some one brought me in a carriage and left me at the church door."

"How long have you been in this condition?"

"For a long time, but for the last two months I have lost the use of my hands."

"What do the doctors say?"

"That they can do nothing for me. Then my relations and friends and the curé of my parish advised me to come and implore the blessing of *Our Lady Help of Christians* who had obtained such wonderful cures."

"Kneel down."

This he did with great difficulty, aided by those present.

Don Bosco gave him his blessing; then said,

"If you have faith in Mary, open your hand."

"I cannot."

"Yes, you can; begin by stretching out your thumb."

He tried, and succeeded.

"Now the first finger."

He put it out, and all the others in succession in the same way.

Then, overcome with joy, he made the sign of the cross, crying out,

"The Mother of God has obtained for me this grace!"

"If the Mother of God has obtained for you this grace, render glory to God by standing on your feet."

He attempted to rise by the aid of his crutch, but Don Bosco said,

"You ought to rise without a crutch, to show your confidence in Mary."

This he immediately did. The curvature of the spine as well as the contraction of his limbs disappeared, he stood erect, and took long strides across the sacristy.

"My friend, go now and testify your gratitude to the Blessed Virgin by making a genuflection before the Blessed Sacrament."

This he did with perfect ease.

"My God! my God! and to think how

long I have been deprived of the use of my body and limbs. Good *Lady Help of Christians*, pray for me."

"My friend, promise me that for the future you will have great devotion to the Blessed Virgin, and that you will be a good Christian."

"I promise, and next Sunday I will go to confession and Communion."

Saying this he took his crutch, and shouldering it as if it were a musket, he walked off deliberately, without saying a word to any one.

It was supposed that he would return at least to give thanks to God.

But this fine fellow had obtained his cure through the intercession of Our Lady Help of Christians, and considered that his campaign was over, and never returned.

CURE OF A SICK WOMAN AND THE CONVERSION OF A CITY.

T. PIERRE D'ARÈNE is a city in Italy where for years Our Lord was little loved.

One curé was more than sufficient to do the duty of the parish, containing thirty thousand souls, and the church was almost deserted.

In consequence of this infidelity three Masonic lodges were proudly throned in their midst, and their pernicious influence destroyed all the germs of good in the country.

The wife of a railroad official and the mother of five very interesting children fell seriously ill.

The doctors having pronounced her case hopeless, the curé proposed to give her the last Sacraments. The sick woman demurred a little, and although she had not been heretofore a very practical Catholic, declared she would confess to no one but

Don Bosco, to which her husband, though a perfect unbeliever, made no objection.

The curé availing himself of this concession, wrote to Don Bosco, who came at once. At that time he contemplated opening a house at St. Pierre d'Arène, and he sought for some providential means to help along the foundation.

The sick woman seemed much gratified when he entered her room. Don Bosco consoled her and assured her that *Our Lady Help of Christians* would certainly cure her, if she asked it with faith; then he heard her confession. "With regard to Communion," added he, "it is much better to receive in church. I will be here for some days, and will pray for you and ask my children to do so; besides, I will say Mass for your intention. Come some morning to Mass and I will give you Communion."

At these words a murmur of surprise and indignation escaped the husband.

"Monsieur l'Abbé," said he, "this is no time to jest: do you not see that this woman is dying, unable even to move from her bed? How can you talk of her going to church?"

"Our Lady Help of Christians has great

power," replied Don Bosco, unmoved. "Let us pray to her together," and the husband knelt with him, to the surprise of everybody, and said the *Our Father*, *Hail Mary*, *Glory be to the Father*, and the *Hail Holy Queen*.

"You must not fail to say these prayers regularly every day till Christmas." It was then the 6th of December. Then putting a medal on the sick woman, and having prevailed on her husband to accept one also, Don Bosco departed.

The woman at once felt a change, the pain ceased, the fever left her, and she was cured. A few days afterwards the railroad official and his wife were at the church at a very early hour, when the invalid made a fervent thanksgiving, and received Holy Communion from the hands of Don Bosco.

This sudden and unhoped-for cure resulted in the speedy conversion of the husband, who enthusiastically declared that the presence of Don Bosco at St. Pierre d'Arène had restored to him his wife and his peace of heart.

The influence of this cure extended further still. The city was deeply moved by it, and it effected a complete transformation in the minds of the people.

Wonderful conversions resulted from it; the church was again filled, and the people returned in such numbers that three priests came to the assistance of the good curé, whose heart overflowed with joy.

Soon another Salésian Institute was founded in this city, and a house was given to Don Bosco, to which the children flocked in great numbers. A large church has since been built and opened to the public, at which ten Salésian priests officiate with much consolation and great benefit to souls.

It is worthy of notice that the Hospital of St. Vincent de Paul of St. Pierre d'Arène and the church are situated in the very midst of the Masonic lodges—a flaming torch dissipating the darkness of error.

A VOCATION AND CURE.

IN 1868 a young man living near Fenestrelles had just finished his year of philosophy. His inclination led him to take holy orders; but he was an orphan, and his grandfather, who was head of the family, decided that his grandson should become a merchant. All the necessary preliminaries had been arranged, and a place was secured for him in a business house in Lyons.

The following Saturday was fixed as the day for his departure. On Monday two friends came to take him to see Don Bosco, who had just arrived in the country. These two friends were in their second year at the seminary, and had heard so much of Don Bosco they had a great desire to see him; but the other young man did not even know his name: he went merely to satisfy his friends. As soon as the three young men were admitted, Don Bosco, scarcely noticing the two seminarians, went directly to the young man about to become a merchant, looked at him in the most friendly manner, then taking his hand, said, " This is a bird we must cage."

The young man was deeply impressed, without knowing exactly why. He felt the desire to follow his vocation very strongly awakened: a desire which, though stifled for a time, was never extinct. A short conversation with Don Bosco ended by confirming his unalterable resolution to consecrate himself to God, and the grandfather, suddenly changing his mind, made no objection and gave his consent.

At that same time two little sisters, of six and eight years, who were almost blind, were brought to Don Bosco. One could barely see the light; the other had chronic inflammation of the eyes, which closed the eyelids so firmly, that her father, a strong, hardy farmer, with all his strength could not open them.

Don Bosco advised them to make a novena to *Our Lady Help of Christians, an Our Father, Hail Mary, Glory be to the Father*, and *Hail Holy Queen* three times a day; and he charged a young student to direct the mother and children in saying these prayers.

The two little girls recovered their sight the very day the novena finished. One was completely cured; there remained on one of the eyes of the other whose lids had been closed a small spot, which, however, did not interfere with her sight.

The young man who had said the novena with them was a witness of the instantaneous cure. He became a priest of the Oratory of St. Francis de Sales, and is one of Don Bosco's favorite sons. He is called Don Ronchail, and is now at the head of the house of St. Pierre, at Nice, the first foundation made by Don Bosco in France.

HOW COUNT C. ENTERED HOLY ORDERS AT THE AGE OF SIXTY-THREE.

COUNT C. was a pious man of the world, and a widower. His only son being married, he found himself in his declining years perfectly independent, and decided to devote the remainder of his life to good works. He consulted Don Bosco as to the best course to pursue. "Become a Salésian priest" was the advice he received.

This answer surprised him very much: he had not the slightest inclination to the life; and to begin the studies for the priesthood at sixty years of age seemed to him beyond his power.

However, having a great veneration for Don Bosco, he took his advice into consideration, and finally familiarized himself somewhat with this novel prospect.

But nature winced a little at the idea, and he saw good reasons for not following this counsel. "After all, how do I know that Don Bosco is not mistaken. He certainly has lights, but his great desire to recruit priests for his Oratory may well mislead him on this subject. I do not wish to lightly take upon myself so serious an obligation. I will consider it." On the morning of the 26th of May, 1877, he went, as he often did, to the Oratory.

The room adjoining Don Bosco's little reception-room was full of people who had been there since early morning, each one going in turn to see him. Count C. took his place in line, and as he had to wait a long time, he entertained himself by watching with curious interest his two neighbors.

Beside him was a poor mother holding on her lap a child of about twelve, evidently in terrible pain; great drops of perspiration covered her face, and her suffering seemed to be increasing so much, that the wearied mother started to go home and went towards the door, supporting her child, who walked with great difficulty.

The assistants observing her, asked why she left without seeing Don Bosco.

"Alas!" she replied, "I cannot wait longer, my child is in such pain, and I am absolutely obliged to be at home at this hour. However, I would not detain Don Bosco long: I only want to ask him in charity to obtain for my poor child the blessing of the Blessed Virgin." Then she told that her child was paralyzed, added to which she had within the last month entirely lost her speech. The child only answered the questions asked her by a motion of the head, being unable to utter a word.

The people, moved with compassion, with

one accord yielded the first place to this interesting sufferer.

It was evident to all that without a miracle this poor child could not be cured, at least immediately. A sudden thought came to the Count's mind.

Raising his soul to the Blessed Virgin, he begged her to give him by a miracle a striking proof of his vocation, and then he would no longer hesitate to do what Don Bosco advised.

A few moments after the little girl and her mother were admitted to the reception-room, and they were there scarcely twelve or fifteen minutes when they appeared accompanied by Don Bosco. The mother shedding tears of joy, the little girl completely transformed, walked without the least difficulty, and said aloud, "The blessed Virgin has just obtained for me this grace." A perfect cure, for the paralyzed arm was as strong as ever and as free in its movements; her speech had also returned.

A grace equally singular removed all hesitation on the part of Count C., and he is now a priest of the Oratory of St. Francis de Sales.

The little girl who was the recipient of such a signal favor consecrated herself later to her who had obtained her cure. She became a member of the Salésian family as a daughter of *Mary Help of Christians*.

PROVIDENCE IS A GOOD BANKER.

WHAT charming things we might relate if we were to tell of the thousand and one circumstances under which Don Bosco received, in the most unexpected and often in the strangest way, the exact sums he needed, and frequently on the day and at the hour they were due, as if the most punctual banker had charge of his affairs!

I will give a few instances selected at random. The house at Turin owed the contractor thirty thousand francs, and he began to be very angry at the delay in the payment. One morning he came to the Oratory in a great rage, prepared to make a scene. He went to the prefect and declared he would not go away until he had received the amount due him. The prefect assured him that he had not a cent in the treasury.

"I am not to be put off in that way," replied the contractor in an angry tone; "I must speak to Don Bosco."

He was conducted to a room where a great many persons awaited their turn to see Don Bosco, and seated himself in a very bad humor, grumbling aloud.

Meanwhile a man of imperious bearing entered, speaking brusquely and impatiently.

"I wish to see Don Bosco at once."

"Will you be seated and wait a few moments? You must take your turn."

"I have not time to wait."

And without further formality he went and knocked at the door where Don Bosco was in conference with some one.

Don Bosco opened the door: "What do you wish, my friend?"

"Father, I wish to speak to you."

"You must take your turn, please; I cannot receive you before all these people who have been here so long."

"I am in a hurry, and what I have to say to you will not take long."

In the face of such persistence Don Bosco

asked the others if he might be allowed to see this person; who, without waiting an answer, walked directly into the room.

His brusque, rather harsh tone did not reassure Don Bosco, who said, "Be seated, I pray you."

"I do not wish to sit down."

"Then tell me what brought you here."

"It is not of much account; it will only take a minute. Here; will you take this?" and he laid a little package on the table and left the room, saying, "Good-by, Father; pray for me."

The Countess V. then entered: "Nothing has happened to you, Father? That man really frightened me; he acted so singularly I was afraid that he would do you some harm."

"No great harm," said Don Bosco, smiling. "Here is what he came to bring me;" and unfolding the little package he found it contained thirty thousand francs.

When the contractor came in his turn Don Bosco gave him the thirty thousand francs due him.

The man, rather confused at having insisted so much, made many excuses.

"Father, I was told you had not wherewith to pay me; they were evidently mistaken."

At one time the Oratory owed three hundred and twenty-five francs for taxes; the time allowed for the payment expired on that very day at noon, and if the small sum was not deposited the collector would be obliged to commence proceedings—that is, to prosecute them.

Don Rua went to the treasurer; he searched the cash-box, but there was not a cent to be found in the house. He went to Don Bosco's room, explained the state of affairs, and asked if he had that amount.

"I have absolutely nothing," replied Don Bosco; "let us pray to *Our Lady Help of Christians;*" and he went quietly on with his work.

A few minutes afterwards there was a knock, and a gentleman asked to see Don Bosco. He was admitted, and after a short conversation said, "Father, I am not rich, but I have here a very small sum which I saved up for your children. Will you accept this modest offering?"

"Most willingly," replied Don Bosco.

The gentleman handed him a small paper, which contained exactly three hundred and twenty-five francs. Don Bosco smiled, and said, "Will you oblige me by giving this to Don Rua as you go out?"

Don Rua, looking at the money, said, "The Father has counted closely; this is just the sum we need;" and he quickly despatched a messenger with it to the Tax Office.

It was then past noon and the warrant had already been sent out, but the messenger had by chance been delayed, and it was recalled without any trouble.

He who acted as the agent of Divine Providence on this occasion afterwards became a Salésian priest.

In March, 1880, Don Bosco went to spend a week in Nice. On this occasion Mr. Ernest Harmel regaled all the children of the house of St. Pierre with a good dinner, to which several members of the Salésian family were invited.

A short time before dinner, Mr. Michel, a lawyer well known for his zeal in all good works, was talking with Don Bosco, who in the course of the conversation said to him, "Our chapel is too small, and very inconvenient; we must absolutely have a better dwelling for Our Lord. Here is a plan which our excellent, worthy architect Mr. Levrot has just handed me; the estimate for the building is thirty thousand francs."

"Thirty thousand francs! I doubt, Father, if you could find that amount at this moment in Nice. We have had so many charitable appeals this winter, so many lotteries, and so many collections of all kinds, the treasury is almost exhausted."

"Nevertheless I must have that amount this very day."

Meanwhile twelve o'clock struck and they all went to table. At dessert, the notary of the house, Mr. Sajetto, rose and said,

"Father, I wish to tell you that a charitable person has sent me, for you, thirty thousand francs. You will find it in my study when you want it."

"Praised be *Our Lady Help of Christians*," said Don Bosco, joining his hands and raising his eyes to heaven; "this is the beginning."

As to the lawyer, he was perfectly astounded at Don Bosco's receiving the exact sum that he had asked for a few moments before.

Don Bosco himself, at a recent conference held at Lyons, told how one day he had to pay at five o'clock fifteen thousand francs to a contractor for work done on the Church of the Sacred Heart at Rome.

At half-past four he still had nothing, when an ecclesiastic came in unexpectedly, bringing the exact sum. He was not to have come that day, but in consequence of some misunderstanding he took the train, he knew not why, and started on the journey almost against his will.

O Blessed Providence! this is one of thy merciful interventions.

The supernatural is denied; but it is everywhere, in us, around us; we are enveloped in it; but alas! our eyes are so fixed on earthly things they see not the light.

AN OPPORTUNE CLAP OF THUNDER.

HERE came a time when the Oratory of St. Francis de Sales, established in the basement of Pinardi's building, could not accommodate the numbers of children who crowded there on Sundays and feast-days. Don Bosco felt the necessity of opening a second Oratory, which was afterwards the Oratory of St. Louis.

After searching for a long time, he finally found a place which seemed to him suitable, and he sought the owner, a Madame Vaglienti, to ask if she would rent it to him.

The woman agreed, but the rent she asked was entirely beyond the poor priest's means. He reasoned with her, tried to interest her in the work; but to no avail: the obstinate owner was inflexible in her demands.

During this discussion the sky became overcast, and suddenly a frightful clap of thunder shook the house and extinguished the lamp in the room.

The woman, crazed with fear, immediately changed her tone: "Good Father, obtain for me that I may escape being struck by lightning, and I will do all you ask of me."

"Thank you," replied Don Bosco. "I will pray God to protect you now and forever."

The thunder ceased, the sky cleared almost immediately, to the delight of the woman, who made no further objection to the price Don Bosco offered her.

A CHARITABLE SPIRIT.

WHILE at Nice, in March, 1880, Don Bosco called a meeting of the Cooperators, which was held in the modest room then used as a chapel at the Patronage of St. Pierre.

Notwithstanding the narrow limits of the place, the meeting was a large and distinguished assemblage, and the good Father having given a very interesting account of his work and of the results obtained therefrom, deigned to make a collection himself for his children.

A gentleman put a gold piece on the plate. "God will return it to you," said Don Bosco in a loud voice. "Oh! if that is the case," said the gentleman, adding another gold piece, "let Him return me a little more."

A BARGAIN.

THE Marquis de X. said one day to Don Bosco, "Father, I would like to give something to your work, but it is impossible for me to do so just now, for a debt of twenty thousand francs, upon which I counted, is, I have just heard, irrevocably lost."

"Those who have given you the information may be mistaken?"

"No, my men of business are very skilful, and they write me there is not the slightest hope of recovering it."

"And if you should recover this sum what would you do?"

"Oh! I promise to give you half of what I receive, my good Father; but I do not think it possible to recover any of it."

"Who knows! it is for the children; I will have them pray for it."

A few days after the Marquis' attorney sent him five thousand francs, recovered, he said, in the most unexpected manner, and later five thousand francs more, then finally the entire sum.

The Marquis faithfully remitted to Don Bosco the ten thousand francs he promised him.

HOW ALMIGHTY GOD PUNISHED THE INGRATITUDE SHOWN TO DON BOSCO AND THOSE WHO TRIED TO THWART HIM.

WE have seen how Don Bosco, having to give up the Refuge Chapel, obtained from the municipality the use of St. Martin's Church, called of the Mills.

The only playground the children had here was a public square in front of the church, and their noise so annoyed the neighbors they complained to the city authorities, who ordered Don Bosco to go elsewhere.

The person chiefly instrumental in Don Bosco's removal was a secretary of the owners of the mills. He libelled these poor children in a paper, in which he heaped up many false statements and ridiculed facts in the most indelicate manner.

These, however, were the last lines he ever wrote: his right hand was struck with palsy, he became weak and languid, and died after three years of suffering.

After leaving St. Martin's the Oratory was moved to *St. Pierre-es-Liens*, a large, convenient place.

We have already spoken of the unfortunate Rector, who had retired to the presbytery adjoining the church, and who had the children immediately sent away because they disturbed his rest.

This poor old man only did this at the instigation of his servant, a violent, cross-grained creature, whom the invasion of what she considered her domain threw into a perfect rage. She went so far as to abuse Don Bosco in the middle of a sermon he was giving to his children, shaking her fist at him, and uttering the most injurious reproaches. Then she urged her master so, and flew into such a rage at "this band of good-for-nothings," that he wrote to complain of them.

This unfortunate letter had scarcely been sent off when the old priest was struck with apoplexy; and two days afterwards his servant followed him to the grave.

The Marquis de Cavour, Chief of the Municipal Police of Turin, twice tried to have the Oratory closed. Scarcely had he made the second attempt when he was taken with an unusually violent attack of gout. He never left his bed again, and died a short time afterwards.

The Marquis and Marchioness of X., of Turin, had been married ten years, but having no children, a great family was thus threatened with extinction. They regretted this extremely, and finally implored Don Bosco to obtain for them the blessing they so much desired.

Don Bosco had all his Oratory pray, and he prayed himself, making a special novena, which was heard, and the Marchioness became the mother of a beautiful boy.

His birth was the occasion of great feasts and all sorts of rejoicing, but the poor children of Valdoco were completely forgotten.

A few years passed, and Don Bosco thought no more of this ingratitude. However, one day, being greatly pressed for funds, and not knowing where to procure daily bread for his numerous family, he presented himself at the house of the Marchioness.

But he was not admitted.

He made a second attempt, was received, and told the object of his visit.

"Monsieur l'Abbé, I regret sincerely that it is not in my power to come to your assistance just now. This is a hard year, and I have very many demands; but I will avail myself of the first opportunity of being of use to you. I am very much engaged to-day, but I will come to see you before long."

The promised visit was made a short time afterwards, but this time it was to implore Don Bosco's help. He was in his room when the door suddenly opened, and the Marquis and his wife entered, in tears. "Father, good Father, do come to our aid! Our child is dying of croup; come and save him."

Don Bosco was preparing to go with them when a servant appeared, saying the child had just breathed his last.

WHAT CAME OF AN ATTEMPT TO PUT DON BOSCO IN AN INSANE ASYLUM.

DON BOSCO was at one time supposed to be deranged. He planned the building of an Oratory, capable of accommodating an immense number of children, with workshops of all kinds, study-rooms, large courts, a chapel, etc.

Such an undertaking would require large sums of money, and it was known that he had no resources. Evidently such a project could only come from the illusions of a disordered brain.

Some of his friends deserted him; others were of opinion that he ought to be placed under a doctor's care, and it seemed to them most advisable that he should be placed for a short time in an insane retreat. He might compromise the clergy, or at least expose himself to ridicule; then hesitation was no longer possible.

The director of the Retreat was forewarned, and was told to be very gentle, but if necessary, very firm with the poor invalid.

It only remained to bring him to the Retreat, and this is the way it was accomplished:

Two ecclesiastics procured a closed carriage and sought Don Bosco in his little room, where they found him.

They talked with him for a while, and did not find it difficult to draw him out on the subject in which he was most particularly interested.

"Monsieur l'Abbé, you would like to build an Oratory?"

Don Bosco had no objection to speak to them of his projects, and of the good which he hoped would be realized.

In a few minutes the two ecclesiastics exchanged significant glances, which plainly said, "There is no longer any doubt of it: he is really crazy."

"Monsieur l'Abbé, we have below a nice carriage; will you take a drive with us?"

Don Bosco appeared not to have the least suspicion of their intention, and when they repeated their invitation he finally accepted. The carriage was at the door.

"Enter, Monsieur l'Abbé."

"Not at all; after you, gentlemen."

"We beg you will enter first?"

"I will do nothing of the kind. I know too well the respect I owe you; after you."

Tired of this formality, the two ecclesiastics entered the carriage, but, instead of following them, Don Bosco quickly slammed the door, and called out to the driver in a stentorian voice, "To the Retreat."

The coachman had had his instructions, and with a vigorous crack of his whip started his horses and never drew rein till he was within the court of the Retreat, the gate of which stood wide open but closed immediately after them, and the director appeared, followed by two nurses.

The two ecclesiastics stepped out, choking with anger, and furiously berated the driver for his stupidity.

"There, there, calm yourself," said the director; "I was told there was only one coming, but we have room for two. You will be very comfortable here."

"Insolent fellow. For whom do you take us? You do not know to whom you are speaking. We are persons of position, and we will have you punished for this."

"Bless me! they are violent," replied the director. "Here, take them to their cells, and, if they do not behave, give them the shower-bath and the strait-jacket."

The unfortunate ecclesiastics were appalled, but fortunately thought of appealing to the chaplain, who identified them, and they were set at liberty. But they had a narrow escape and went off in great haste, declaring they would not be caught in that way again.

The laugh was not on their side, and it was well established that if Don Bosco is tainted with the folly of the Cross, he nevertheless possesses a certain amount of innocent mischief, which served on more than one occasion to protect him from the snares of his enemies.

THE COLONEL.

DON BOSCO, when at Rome, was one day crossing the Corso accompanied by his secretary, when a Colonel in uniform met him.

"Monsieur l'Abbé, are you not Don Bosco."

"Why do you ask?"

"I want to know if you are not Don Bosco."

"But why do you wish to know?"

"Really, Monsieur l'Abbé, are you or are you not Don Bosco?"

"I am the person you are asking for." Don Bosco said this in rather a brusque tone, not being perfectly satisfied of the motive of these questions.

But scarcely had he said his name when the Colonel threw himself at his feet in the middle of the street, and taking his hand kissed it, saying, "O my good Father!"

"What is the meaning of this, Colonel?"

"Is it possible, good Father, you do not recognize the little orphan you picked up in the streets in ——, when at the death of his parents he was left destitute, not knowing what was to become of him? For six years you sheltered him and were to him father and mother, and you do not wish him now to express to you his gratitude!"

"What! is it you, you little rascal?" said Don Bosco, smiling, and giving him a tap on the cheek. "It seems to me you have made your way very well in the world."

"Yes, when I left the Patronage I enlisted. Thanks to the education which I received from you, I soon became an officer, and I am now a Colonel."

He would not leave Don Bosco until he had made him promise to dine with him the next day.

He presented him, when he came, to his wife and three beautiful children. It was a very happy home, and Don Bosco returned thanks to *Our Lady Help of Christians* for the marked protection she had granted to one of his orphans.

HOW DON BOSCO MANAGED TO TAKE THE YOUNG CULPRITS IN THE PRISON OF TURIN OUT FOR A HOLIDAY.

DON BOSCO'S numerous duties at the Oratory did not make him forget other works of charity, particularly his visits to the prisons.

He devoted himself in a special manner to the great numbers of young men and children whom he found there, and with a success that afforded his priestly heart much consolation.

A retreat he preached in the prison was followed by an almost general Communion.

Delighted with the good dispositions manifested by the children, he resolved to procure for them as a mark of his approbation some special favor, and he at once decided to ask permission to take them out on a picnic.

The deprivation of liberty and exercise is the hardest and most insupportable punishment to youth. A good run across fields, a whole day spent in the open air, cannot fail to give great pleasure.

Don Bosco went to the superintendent of the prison, and with great simplicity laid before him his request, as if it were the most natural thing in the world.

He asked to be allowed to take the children on an excursion; they were to go in the morning and return in the evening, and he would take the best possible care of them all.

The superintendent started with surprise at this eccentric proposition. "But, Monsieur l'Abbé, do you think the king's soldiers have nothing better to do than to walk after these little vagabonds? And moreover, I am responsible for every escape."

"Who said anything about soldiers? I will take all the responsibility: not one will escape; and I promise to faithfully bring back to you every one of the children you will intrust to my care."

How was it that this extraordinary request was ever granted? It had to be submitted to the Minister Ratizzi, but Don

Bosco seemed to have the power of removing all obstacles.

On the appointed day, after Mass, three hundred and fifty children and youths left the prison in perfect order, led by Don Bosco, calm and smiling.

The royal castle of Stupinigi had been selected as their place for pleasuring. Five leagues there and back was not too much to stretch their young legs after such long inaction.

It would be impossible to describe the joy depicted on every countenance. Moreover, there was not the least disorder, nor fruit stolen, nor a single depredation committed. Their greatest concern was to tenderly care for their good Father: when they noticed that he was tired walking, in the twinkling of an eye they shouldered the provisions which had been carried by the donkey that Don Bosco's thoughtfulness had provided, and they made him mount the animal, which two of the children carefully led by the bridle.

In the evening the superintendent proved by calling the roll that all the children had returned to the prison; not one was missing.

THE SEMINARIAN FRANCIS.

IN 1862 a seminarian became very ill with pleurisy, and one morning, supposing him to be in danger, the Sacraments were administered.

Don Bosco after his Mass came to see him. "Well, Francis, are you sorry to leave this poor world? Do you wish to go, or would you like to remain longer with us?"

"I really do not know, Father," replied Francis; "give me till this evening to consider. Soon after he said to himself, "I was very foolish not to have said that I wished to go to heaven, for Don Bosco would have promised it to me, and I would thus have secured my salvation."

Don Bosco returned in the evening. "Father," said the seminarian eagerly, "I have decided: I prefer to die, if you will promise me that I will go to heaven."

"It is too late, my poor Francis," replied Don Bosco. "You will recover, and you will live for some time, but be prepared to suffer a great deal."

He did in fact recover, but was afflicted with sores on his legs, and had to endure great suffering.

He however became a priest, and did good service, but the sores on his legs never healed, and he suffered till his death, which happened twelve years afterward, in 1874.

A SICK FRIEND.

DON RUA, the incomparable prefect of the Oratory of Turin, was a pupil of Don Bosco, and had been with him since he was nine years of age. It would be difficult to express the love and veneration the pupil had for his master, and how tenderly the master loved his pupil.

In 1868 Don Rua was taken seriously ill. He was exhausted by excessive fatigue caused by his incessant work night and day in the management of the household affairs, for he only allowed himself four hours' sleep. Hence he was soon stricken down with sickness, and the doctors declared that his life was in great danger.

He asked for and received the last Sacraments; but imagine his grief when he learned that Don Bosco was away. Was he to leave this world without seeing him again?

Everybody at the Oratory was very anxious, and great was the relief when Don Bosco, who had been longed for so earnestly, returned. "Hurry, hurry, Father, come to Don Rua: he is very ill, and may pass away at any moment," were the first words that greeted him.

"Oh!" replied Don Bosco, unmoved, "I know Don Rua; he is not a man to go away without my permission." And instead of going to the sick man's room, he went to the chapel and began calmly to hear confessions; then in the evening he took his supper, and returned to his room.

The next morning after his Mass he went to see Don Rua, who had passed a very comfortable night and was convalescent.

A CONFESSION.

A YOUNG boy of Turin wishing to go to confession went one Sunday morning to one of the city parishes and made his confession to a priest whose confessional was so surrounded that it could scarcely be seen. In the afternoon one of his companions took him to the Oratory of St. Francis de Sales, where he had never been before, and he immediately joined the other children at play in the court.

When Don Bosco came he noticed the boy, and patting him caressingly on the head, said, "Come here a minute, little one, and I will hear your confession;" and taking him aside he seated himself, and putting his arm around the boy's neck began to enumerate all the faults the child had committed.

The poor boy, aghast, stood up, and opening his eyes wide said, "But how do you know all this? you must be the priest to whom I went to confession this morning."

"Not at all, my child; do you not see I can read this in your eyes?" he said, giving him a friendly tap on the cheek.

It was well known that Don Bosco had not been out all that day, consequently could not have been in the church where the child went to confession.

A DREAM.

ONE night a young ecclesiastic, who occupied a room near Don Bosco's, noticed that he was very restless in his sleep and that he talked aloud for some time.

The next morning he remarked, "Father, you did not sleep well last night?"

"Yes, I had rather a singular dream. I was in a country where they did not speak Italian, and I saw a house out in the country where children were running about, others were busy at farm labor, and there were Salésian priests among them."

That very day—it was in 1876—Don Bosco received a letter from Mgr. Terris,

Bishop of Frejus and Toulon, offering him a commodious property in Var, near Crau d'Hyères, for the establishment of an agricultural Patronage.

At this time Don Bosco had but one house in France, that of Nice, and he had as yet no agricultural patronage. He did not accept this offer at once; several difficulties arose, and the negotiations lasted for nearly two years. Finally, the foundation was decided upon and carried out. It was intrusted to a Salésian priest, Father Perrot, who installed himself in the property called Navarre on the 5th of July, 1878, and immediately collected as many children as the buildings could accommodate.

In the latter part of January, 1879, Don Bosco made a voyage to Marseilles in the interest of a new foundation, and took occasion on this journey to visit his Patronage at Var, which he had not yet seen. He slept at Hyères, and the next morning was brought to Navarre.

The property is situated about twelve miles from Hyères. It is a very isolated place, but is not devoid of beauty; hills covered with pines and venerable oaks surround the house. In front were vines and wide-spreading lands. But the land at that time was almost entirely uncultivated, and the buildings, formerly farmhouses, were in a very dilapidated condition.

The children, headed by Father Perrot, came to meet Don Bosco, and escorted him to the house singing.

They first went to the little chapel, then to visit the buildings.

When they came to the farm Don Bosco surveyed it attentively. "This is the very place I saw in my dream: I recognize it perfectly; there is no doubt about it."

Father Perrot knew of the dream, and he also remarked the similarity of the details.

It was certainly the place, and Don Bosco declared that he recognized the voice of the child, who sang a motet, as the one he had heard in his dream.

Assuredly Divine Providence destined this place as an asylum for our children. *Praise be to Our Lady Help of Christians.*

PIETY OF DON BOSCO'S CHILDREN.

WHEN Don Bosco was asked to obtain a grace for any one, he generally said, "I will have my children pray for it." Nor was this a vain promise. The prayer of the many assembled together had marvellous effect, and its power was certainly increased by the great piety of many of the children.

For among nearly nine hundred children and youths who were boarders at the Oratory of St. Francis de Sales at Turin there were perhaps a hundred each of whom was a real St. Aloysius; and four or five hundred would make perfect religious. In some of these children the interior life was singularly and strikingly developed, and there were those among them who manifested a supernatural knowledge and foresight. For instance, after Mass one day a child came to Don Bosco and said,

"Father, you are thinking of doing such a thing: you are right; it will succeed?"

"Indeed, little one! how do you know that? who told it to you?"

The child was confused, stammered, and when urged to tell, was silent, and finally even forgot what he was going to say.

Don Bosco has written and published the life of one of his children, Savio Domenico, a pupil of the Oratory of St. Francis de Sales, who was born in 1842 and died in 1857. This child was a perfect model of purity and sanctity. Many graces are said to have been obtained by his prayers during his life.

When he died he became a subject of veneration to his companions. They invoked his aid and precious graces, and remarkable cures were obtained through his intercession.

There were other children also who were favored with supernatural gifts: one of them, Michael Fassio, predicted, a year before it happened, the gunpowder explosion which in 1852 came near destroying the Oratory. He was a locksmith's apprentice and remarkably pious. In 1851 he had a serious attack of illness, which resulted fatally. He received the last Sacraments, and one day, as if under heavenly inspiration, he cried out, "Woe to Turin! woe to Turin!"

"With what are we threatened," asked one of his companions.

"An earthquake."

"When?"

"Next year. Woe to Turin on the 26th of April?"

"What ought we to do?" asked the terrified children.

"Pray to St. Louis to protect the Oratory and all its inmates."

A few days afterward he rendered his soul to God.

On the very day indicated, the 26th of April, 1852, the earth was shaken by the terrible explosion in the powder-mill situated near the Oratory. This catastrophe cost the lives of thirty workmen, and might have completely destroyed not only the Oratory, but also a great part of the city of Turin, had it not been for the heroism of Sergeant Paul Sacchi. This brave man, although wounded, managed to have eight hundred barrels of powder removed from one of the magazines. The children, deeply impressed by Fassio's prediction, followed his advice, and added to their night prayers an *Our Father and Hail Mary* in honor of St. Louis de Gonzaga, with the invocation *Ab omni malo libera nos, Domine* ("From all evil deliver us, O Lord"). This practice is still observed in the Salésian houses.

THE ATTEMPTS TO KILL DON BOSCO.

THE emancipation of the Jews and of the Waldenses by order of Charles Albert in the beginning of 1848 created intense excitement among the different sects. Under political pretexts they aroused the lower classes by spreading false and perfidious accusations against the Catholic clergy, and consequently it was not safe for a minister of God at that time to go through certain of the most peaceful parts of Turin.

Besides this, Don Bosco had aroused much hatred by establishing his Oratory at Valdoco. This quarter, haunted by the worst classes, was the natural resort of people of questionable avocations, and much disturbed by them. Here assembled gamblers, drunkards, and all kinds of evil-doers, as well as strolling musicians, showmen, and every species of vagabond, men ready in the use of the knife, who recoiled at nothing to prevent the invasion of what they considered their domain.

This state of things explains in a measure why they were so furious against the poor priest. One day when he was in the chapel surrounded by his children, to whom he was teaching the Catechism, a shot was fired at him through an open window. The ball passed between his arm and his chest, tearing his *soutane*, and flattened itself against the wall.

The terrified children rose in tumult, but Don Bosco, impassible and smiling, said, "If the Blessed Virgin had not made him miss his aim, he would certainly have hit me, but he did not reach me."

Then looking at his torn *soutane:* "O poor *soutane*," he said, "I am very sorry for what has happened to you, for you are the only one I possess."

On another occasion, when in the midst of his children, an insane man rushed at him with a large knife, and it was only by a miracle that he escaped to his room.

One evening the door-bell rang at the Oratory, and some one begged Don Bosco to come as quickly as possible to administer the Sacraments to a woman in the neighborhood who was dying.

It was a very dark night, and as the Father had recently escaped being killed, there were objections made to his going out; but Don Bosco having declared his determination to go to the sick woman, remonstrance was vain, but four students accompanied him to protect him in case of need.

The little group came to a rather isolated house and two of the young men remained outside, while the other two went up with Don Bosco to the door of the room which he entered alone.

As soon as he came in four stalwart fellows rose and wished him good-day in a tone which they tried to make very gracious. But Don Bosco observed their repulsive appearance, and that they were all armed with clubs, the size of which was not reassuring.

He approached the bed of the supposed sick woman. She looked very well, and had a singularly bright color for one who was dying.

"Well, my good woman, do you want to make your confession?"

"Certainly I do," she replied in a far from feeble voice, "but first that old dotard, that rascal there, my brother-in-law, must beg my pardon;" and she began to pour forth a torrent of abuse.

"Will you hold your tongue, you miserable wretch," shouted one of the men, who with a backward motion of his hand threw the only candle on the floor and extinguished it, thus leaving the room in perfect darkness. At the same time Don Bosco received a blow from a club which would have felled him had it not glanced off his shoulder.

With his usual presence of mind he seized a chair and raised it over his head; the blows fell like hail on this improvised helmet, which protected his head. He was thus able to reach the door, and putting his hand on the latch he threw the chair at his assailants, and opening the door joined the two young men who awaited him outside.

All this was done so quickly that for a moment they were motionless with astonishment.

When they gained the street the young men were terrified to see Don Bosco covered with blood. But fortunately the wound he received was not a serious one; while he was protecting his head with the chair, a blow from a club cut his left thumb to the bone.

Don Bosco had quite recently another narrow escape. In December, 1881, he was in his room at the Oratory of Turin when a well-dressed gentleman who had asked for him was shown in. The visitor began to talk of various things, and gradually grew excited and gesticulated violently. Don Bosco, who watched him attentively, noticed that a six-barrelled revolver had noiselessly slipped from his pocket on to the sofa where they both sat.

Without betraying the least fear Don Bosco adroitly got possession of the revolver and hid it under his *soutane*.

The stranger soon began to feel his pockets, as if searching for something, and to look around the floor.

"What is the matter, my dear sir? have you lost something?"

"Yes, I do not know where I could have put—"

"What?"

"Nothing, nothing."

He searched again, looked under the sofa, and even went into the next room, where Don Bosco's secretary was.

"You have found nothing?"

"No, nothing whatever."

He came back to Don Bosco, who, perfectly unmoved all the time, and looking him in the eyes, drew out the revolver, and pointing it at the breast of the intruder, said,

"This is what you are looking for, is it not?"

The man, much confused, tried to get possession of the revolver, but Don Bosco prevented him, and in forcible language reproved him for his wicked designs.

Ashamed and confounded, the creature finally acknowledged that he had come to kill him, but had now abandoned his sinful design. Don Bosco opened the door, and giving him back his pistol said, " Go, my friend, and may Almighty God enlighten you and deign to have mercy on you!"

In the following chapter we shall see how, on several occasions, Don Bosco's life was protected in a most marvellous manner, and what a singular defender Divine Providence sent him.

DON BOSCO'S DOG.

IN the early days of the Oratory the Valdoco quarter was not as thickly populated as it is now. A few scattered houses and waste lands overgrown with bushes separated the Oratory from the last house in the city. Hence, when Don Bosco was out at night great anxiety was felt concerning him. In returning home he had to cross an almost deserted tract of land very favorable for an attack, and it was well known that there were those who had sworn to take his life. His friends begged him to be cautious; but when there was question of the exercise of his holy ministry, or the interest of his orphans, nothing could restrain him.

On one occasion, when returning rather late from the city, feeling somewhat apprehensive, he hastened his steps, when suddenly a large gray dog stood beside him. At first he was frightened, but soon recovered himself when he saw that the splendid animal showed signs of friendship and walked along with him. The dog accompanied him to the Oratory and then disappeared.

From that time, whenever Don Bosco was obliged to return late from the city, the dog seldom failed to join him after he had passed the last houses, and accompanied him to the door.

Don Bosco soon came to look upon this faithful and valuable companion as a true friend; he called him *Il Grigio* ("The Gray"), on account of his color. On several different occasions the dog evidently saved his life.

One very dark night, when he was returning to the Oratory, he took the road leading from the Consolata to the Cottolengo Hospital, to keep as near as possible to the inhabited parts of the country. At a certain part of the road two men who had followed him for a time suddenly sprung upon him, and while one of them threw a cloak over his head, the other put his hand over his mouth to prevent his calling out.

Don Bosco gave himself up for lost, when suddenly a terrible growl, like that of an angry lion, was heard, and at the same time *Il Grigio* rushed upon the assailants, felling them to the ground in an instant. Don Bosco freed himself from the cloak which almost smothered him, and he saw one of the villains running away as fast as he could; the other was lying on the ground, held there by the dog, who had seized him by the throat.

"Master, master, call off your dog!" implored the poor wretch; "he is choking me."

"I will call him off if you promise to do better for the future."

"Yes, yes; but call him quickly, or I am a dead man."

Don Bosco spoke to the dog, who immediately loosed his hold of the man's throat. The latter, without saying a word, took himself off as fast as he could.

Another evening Don Bosco was returning home by the S. Massino road when an assassin fired twice at him from behind a tree where he was hiding, almost touching him with the muzzle of the pistol; it missed fire both times, the caps only snapping. Then he sprung on Don Bosco, determined to execute his design by other means. But just at that moment *Il Grigio* bounded forward on the murderous villain, threw him to the ground, and put him to flight. Then the dog accompanied Don Bosco to the door of the Oratory.

On another occasion *Il Grigio* delivered his master from a gang of assailants. It was night. Don Bosco was returning by the road that leads from the Emmanuel Philibert Square to the Rondo, when a man with a heavy club suddenly sprung upon him. The place was deserted. Don Bosco tried to escape by flight, but his assailant was too quick for him. He raised his club to strike him, when Don Bosco, urged by imminent danger, gave the fellow a well-directed blow in the stomach that stretched him on the ground, where he lay, crying in pitiable tones, *Ahi! ahi! che son morto!* ("Oh! oh! I am killed!")

Don Bosco thought himself safe, but on all sides men armed with clubs rose from among the bushes. Resistance was no longer possible. At this critical moment a terrible barking announced the arrival of *Il Grigio*, who ran rapidly around his friend to keep off the assailants, howling so furiously and showing such formidable fangs, that the rascals fled in confusion. Thus Don Bosco was again able to return home safe and sound in company with his brave defender.

Another evening Don Bosco was preparing to go out. As it was late, his mother, good Madame Margaret, tried to persuade him not to go; but in vain. On opening the door, he found his dog stretched across the step and he refused to move. He pushed him gently with his foot, saying. "Come, *Grigio*, let me pass."

The dog growled threateningly, but would not stir.

"You see, my son," said Madame Margaret, "the dog has more sense than you. At least take his warning; do not go out."

Don Bosco attempted twice more to pass, but as the dog still refused to make way

way for him, and persisted in his significant growling, he finally gave up the idea and returned quietly to his room.

In less than a quarter of an hour afterwards a neighbor came in great haste to warn Don Bosco to be on his guard, and not to attempt to go out that evening, for he had seen four desperate-looking ruffians hiding in a by-path, and he had overheard them declare that they would surely succeed this time in putting Don Bosco out of the way.

One evening the dog appeared in the court of the Oratory. The children wanted to put him out; but one of the boys exclaiming "It is Don Bosco's dog," they all began at once to play with him. Some climbed on his back, others pulled his ears, and thus conducted him to the Refectory, where Don Bosco was at supper with his mother and several priests.

"It is my *Grigio*," said the Father; and the dog came to him to be petted. *Grigio* walked gravely around the table; Don Bosco and several others offered him bread, meat, and water, but he refused everything. He finally laid his great handsome head on the table, and fixed his eyes affectionately on Don Bosco, as if to wish him good-day.

"Since you will take nothing, you may go," said Don Bosco; and the dog went off with one of the boys, who opened the door for him.

It was soon explained why the dog came that evening. Don Bosco was to return late; but it happened that the Marquis Fassati brought him back in his carriage, so that he was home much earlier than was expected.

Il Grigio doubtless wanted to assure himself that his master was safe at home.

In the autumn of 1866 Don Bosco saw his strange protector for the last time. He was at Murialdo de Castelnuovo, his birthplace, and was to go to one of his friends at Moncucco. But night stole on before he was aware of it, and he had to pass through a dangerous piece of wood.

"Oh! if I only had my *Grigio* with me," he could not help exclaiming.

Immediately the dog was beside him and accompanied him to his destination. Don Bosco was not attacked that night by his enemies, but *Il Grigio* did him good service by driving off two large mastiffs who had been left to guard a vineyard. He had been told they were dangerous to passers-by, and they did actually jump at him, but *Il Grigio* gave them such a warm reception that they went off howling with pain.

On his arrival, the guests who awaited supper for him were delighted with the beauty of the dog. " What a splendid dog you have ! we have never seen one like him; he must be some very rare breed !" They offered the dog all kinds of delicacies, but he would not touch anything.

Some of the young men, surprised at this obstinate refusal to eat, resolved to lock him up in a room.

When he has fasted for twelve hours, they said, he must eat and drink.

Next day they went to look after their captive, but to their great surprise the dog had disappeared, though the windows and doors were carefully fastened.

It was never discovered whence the dog had come, or whither he had gone after his mission was fulfilled. No one ever heard anything more of him.

THE CONFESSION OF A THIEF.

DON BOSCO, returning from one of his journeys, had to pass through a small wood. It was just at nightfall, and the place was very lonely. Suddenly an armed man rushed upon him, and demanded his purse or his life.

"As to purse, I have none," replied Don Bosco, "and my life God gave me, and He alone has the right to take it from me."

"Come, Abbé, less ceremony; your purse, or I will strike."

Just then Don Bosco recognized in his assailant one of the prisoners to whom he had formerly taught Catechism in the prison at Turin.

"What! is it you? such a one?" said he. "I must admit that you keep your promises very badly, and that you follow a very bad trade. I had so much confidence in you, but how you have disappointed me!"

The thief also recognized with whom he was dealing, and hung his head in pain and confusion.

"Really, Father, I did not know it was

you; you may be sure I would have left you in peace."

"This will not do, my child; you must absolutely change your life. You try the patience of God, and if you do not repent at once, take care lest you may not have time for repentance at the hour of death."

"I certainly will change my life, good Father, I promise you."

"You must go to confession."

"I will."

"When will you go?"

"Oh! very soon."

"Then come now; that is best: kneel there."

And seating himself on a large stone, Don Bosco pointed to a place at his feet.

After a few moments' hesitation, the man knelt down. Don Bosco, putting his arm around his neck, as he used to do, and pressing him to his heart, heard his confession. Then he embraced him, and giving him a medal of *Our Lady Help of Christians* and the small amount of money he had with him, Don Bosco went on, accompanied by the thief as far as the gates of the city. This man became afterwards a very good citizen.

DON BOSCO.

WILL tell you a story, ladies,—listen it is not long,
Of love divine and durable, adorable and strong,
Which pierced and filled with sudden flame an humble priest of God.
There were children of the Crucified, whose feet had only trod
The lonesome paths of misery,—the children of the street;
He took them to his wounded heart, and in the glowing heat
Of charity ineffable, deprived of power or pelf,
He gave them all he had to give,—the god-like gift, himself!

The mighty hand of God he knew would strengthen and protect,
The Spirit of the Holy One, would counsel and direct
The friend of helpless infancy, and give into his hand
The splendor of the kingdoms and the riches of the land.
This Abbé poor and humble, with a single child began
His work of prayer and patience, and, as Heaven blest his plan,

Another and another, till the glorious array
Of eighty thousand little ones rejoice his Home
to-day.*
Yes, eighty thousand children is the number that I
give:
He cherished them, and nourished them, and taught
them how to live.
And, brave and happy workers, right merrily they
laughed,
As they grew strong in health and frame, and skilled
in handicraft.
But oh! how far beyond it all! he taught them each to
know
The deathless beauty of the soul, surpassing all
below.
These children of the people, thus ennobled in their
turn
With quenchless fire of charity, their hearts began to
burn
With quenchless fire of charity enkindled from above.
They listed in his army, young evangelists of love;
They knew the Master workman, the Boy of Bethlehem.
O sweet contagion of the heart! O glorious thing
for them!
Six thousand priests anointed, young soldiers strong
and bold,
Now pray for their protectors and the founder of their
fold.

---

* Since this was written the number of children has increased to one hundred thousand.

Yes, eighty thousand little ones! Why, ladies, they must eat,
And not a little truly; for, let me here repeat,
Although a child an angel is, his appetite is good,
And while upon the earth he needs both bed and roof and food.
This truth appears, as now to us, with melancholy force,
When'er an empty purse remains a last and sad resource.
When children cry with hunger dire some friend for them must ask;
And who if not the Virgin Blest shall undertake the task?
O Mother of the motherless, strong helper of the weak!
O ye who help her little ones! what favor would ye seek?
O happy benefactors by her gentle grace beguiled,
She gives you for your guerison the Only one—the Child.

. . . .

And thus the priest, the penniless, what treasure does he hold?
It is the Queen of Heaven high who furnishes the gold.
A stick and sack the Apostles held for miracles and cures;
'Tis all he has except a purse—and that, dear friends, is yours!

Espiney	BQX
AUTHOR	7717
Don Bosco	.E86
TITLE	

Espiney   BQX
                                  7717
Don Bosco   .E86 .

www.ingramcontent.com/pod-product-compliance
Lightning Source LLC
Chambersburg PA
CBHW020253170426
43202CB00008B/349